THEATERS
of the
BODY

Books by Joyce McDougall

Dialogue With Sammy (with S. Lebovici)
A Plea for a Measure of Abnormality
Theaters of the Mind

A NORTON PROFESSIONAL BOOK

THEATERS
of the
BODY

A PSYCHOANALYTIC APPROACH
TO PSYCHOSOMATIC ILLNESS

Joyce McDougall

W· W· *Norton & Company* · *New York* · *London*

Printed in the United States of America.

First Edition

Library of Congress Cataloging-in-Publication Data

McDougall, Joyce.
  Theaters of the body : a psychoanalytic approach to psychosomatic
illness / Joyce McDougall. — 1st ed.
    p. cm.
  Bibliography: p.
  Includes index.
  1. Somatoform disorders. 2. Alexithymia. 3. Psychoanalysis.
4. Medicine, Psychosomatic. I. Title.
RC552.H8M36 1989   89-9410
616.89′17—dc20   CIP

ISBN 0-393-70082-8

W. W. Norton & Company, Inc., 500 Fifth Avenue, New York, N.Y. 10110
W. W. Norton & Company Ltd., 37 Great Russell Street, London WC1B 3NU

1 2 3 4 5 6 7 8 9 0

To my husband Sidney Stewart, without whose constant caring, criticisms, and encouragement this book might not have been written.

Contents

INTRODUCTION

The Psychosoma and the Psychoanalytic Voyage

W HY "THEATERS OF THE BODY" as a title? While writing *Theaters of the Mind* (McDougall, 1982a), I slowly became aware, as so often happens when one is writing, that a further book was developing out of the one in which I was involved. In choosing the theater as a metaphor for psychic reality, I was perhaps following in the steps of Anna O who, at the turn of the century, referred to her free associations during her therapy with Breuer (Breuer and Freud, 1893–1895), as her "private theater." My first challenge was an attempt at understanding the underlying meaning of the complex psychic scenarios that give rise to sexual deviations (McDougall, 1964). Even then I became aware that the creation of inner "theater scripts," which, though written in early childhood, have a lasting effect on the adult mind, extended also to neurotic and to psychosomatic manifestations. I had also observed among patients who were neither neurotic, nor psychotic, nor sexually deviant, another elusive manifestation that I called "pseudo-normality"; this led to the publication in 1978 of *A Plea for a Measure*

1

of Abnormality. Later, when I came to write *Theaters of the Mind* I was concerned with sorting out the different places in which the mind's "I" plays out its hidden dramas, along with the accompanying scenarios, and characters, that make up the psychic repertory. Having dealt with what I called the "neurotic theater," followed by the "psychotic," the "transitional," and the "narcissistic" theaters, I found myself struggling with a theater that I named, provisionally, "the psychosoma on the psychoanalytic stage." This proved to be too vast a subject to be enclosed within *Theaters of the Mind*, and, in fact, threatened to take over the whole book. It is evident that "Theaters of the Body" had been claiming my attention as a title long before I began writing the book.

So I am now ready to give a more comprehensive view of the body's "theaters," focusing on the understanding and exploration of psychosomatic phenomena in a psychoanalytic setting. Originally I had believed that in psychosomatic states the body was reacting to a psychological threat as though it were a physiological one; that there was a severe split between psyche and soma and that this was due to our patients' unawareness of their emotional states in threatening situations. The curtains on the mind's stage were tightly drawn, so to speak; no sound reached the outside ears, and yet a drama was being played out in this secret theater that threatened the very life of the theater owner himself.

Consider this situation: After years of difficult, though to all appearances successful work, I terminated analysis with an alcoholic patient. He went on to build an international reputation for his creativity and as he rose in fame, to become a happy ambassador for psychoanalysis. Then, after years had gone by, he returned to announce that he was dying—dying of a cancer of the throat whose earlier symptoms were not revealed in the theaters of his mind. The curtains had been kept down, the words muffled, so that no warning was audible—warning that, had it been heard, might have saved his life!

All of us have heard of such occult dramas being played out on the theaters of our patients' minds. Indeed, we are often vaguely, and anxiously, aware of them, not only among our analysands but also among our colleagues, our friends, or our family.

Therefore, in this book we shall look not only at people who react to psychological distress through psychosomatic manifestations, but also at the psychosomatic potentiality or part of every individual. We all tend to somatize at those moments when inner or outer circumstances overwhelm our habitual psychological ways of coping. It also commonly happens that certain psychosomatic phenomena, as well as recurrent tendencies to fall ill physically, disappear as an unanticipated side-effect of psychoanalytic treatment, sometimes without specific exploration of the underlying significance of such illnesses in the psychic economy.

However, it should be emphasized that analysts would not normally accept people for psychoanalytic therapy solely on the basis of psychosomatic complaints. Although these might well be a reflection of psychological suffering, they are not necessarily an indication for analysis. A psychoanalytic adventure is undertaken by those interested in charting the unmapped continents of their minds. Individuals engaging in such an expedition do so with the hope that their discoveries may enable them to profit from the adventure of living, and better weather the storms and disappointments that each lifetime inevitably brings. As with all journeys, before one starts a plan has to be formulated and discussed with those who are to accompany one on the voyage; decisions must be made as to whether a therapeutic challenge can be adequately met by psychoanalytic treatment. Sometimes people set out on the wrong journey.

THE BEGINNING OF THE VOYAGE

Let us listen to Mr. Z, who has suffered for more years than he cares to remember from intractable insomnia for which no medical cause can be found. A traditional psychoanalyst may propose that insomnia of this kind indicates that the patient, even though exhausted, is afraid to fall asleep, afraid of the dreams he might have, afraid to give up his grasp of the day and the external world. The analyst might further propose that the hidden reasons for these fears could be uncovered through analytic exploration. A psychiatrist, on the other hand, may propose an efficient soporific that will guarantee Mr. Z five or six hours of restful sleep and a feeling of being ready to face the day on awakening. Depending on his character makeup, Mr. Z may say to the analyst, "I don't care what's *causing* my insomnia; all I want is to get rid of it!," or to the psychiatrist, "I don't want to be drugged all my life in order to sleep, I want to understand *why* I can't just fall asleep like other people!" Obviously, there is a risk that Mr. Z, if not carefully heeded as to the true nature of his quest, may find himself engaged in a treatment that later—perhaps years later—he will come to question or regret.

Clearly, in Mr. Z's scenario we are faced with two quite different types of demand for help. The consulting psychiatrist who treats with medication or the consulting psychoanalyst who relies on the analytic method as the curative tool is called upon to discover what the *patient* is actually seeking. The psychiatrist hopes that carefully prescribed medication will allow the symptoms from which the patient is suffering to be stabilized, while the psychoanalyst hopes that the analysand's increased self-knowledge will reduce the tendency to symptom repetition and lead to more creative ways of investing psychic energy. Since, as analysts recognize, psychoanalysis is not necessarily the treatment of choice for all psychological or psychosomatic disorders, this question of choice, from a psychoanalytic viewpoint, merits further attention.

WHAT IS A "PSYCHOANALYTIC" REQUEST FOR HELP?

How does one evaluate a demand for psychoanalytic treatment? Since in the first interview the analyst is implicitly called upon to make a judgment of the potential patient's search for help it is important to determine exactly what has to be weighed. While recognizing that different analysts have different ways of approaching preliminary interviews, I shall give my own perspective on this complex question. What do I want to know? How do I go about getting the information I need? And how do I evaluate it?

Whether the future analysand suffers from psychosomatic maladies, from neurotic, psychotic or character symptoms, or from addictive problems, my approach remains the same. Symptoms tell us very little about a prospective analysand's chances of being helped by some form of psychoanalytic therapy. Every analyst has had the experience of accepting in treatment someone who appeared (according to the theories and according to clinical experience) eminently suitable for psychoanalytic treatment — only to discover a year or two later that the patient is still at the stage of preliminary interviews. To my mind there are several basic requirements that constitute an acceptable plea for psychological help. And they are not always in evidence in the first interview! Let us review these briefly.

1. Awareness of Psychic Suffering

It may seem self-evident that a would-be patient is suffering *psychologically*; otherwise why would he have come to see a psychoanalyst? But this condition is not always present. Let us consider a few common examples.

A number of people seek help solely in order to please someone else. For example, the marriage partner or lover may say that he/she will not go on with this relationship unless the other "does something" about his/her problems. Or the family doctor might advise psychoanalysis. This is frequently the case with people suffering from maladies commonly accepted as being of psychosomatic origin. (Mrs. A, discussed in Chapter 4, is a case in point.) However, a number of psychosomatic sufferers are totally unaware of any mental pain and may deny any potential relationship between physical suffering and psychological distress. To engage such an individual in psychoanalytic therapy might prove not only useless but positively dangerous. When a patient adamantly claims only physical suffering and displays no awareness of any psychological suffering, it is possible that he or she has come to the wrong door.

Another example involves candidates of psychoanalytic training institutes who are required to undertake a personal analysis. While personal analysis is an essential experience for anyone who hopes to practice psychoanalysis or psychoanalytic therapy, an educational requirement does not in itself constitute an acceptable reason for engaging in an analytic venture. It is, of course, evident that the future psychoanalyst adds to the wish to understand personal psychological problems the hope that because of personal analytic experience, he or she will be able not only to better understand and help others, but also to protect them from being affected adversely by his or her own personal problems or frailties.

In sum, it is essential that all would-be analysands, whatever their source of referral, *wish to undertake analysis for themselves.* If there is no recognition of psychological suffering, such seekers are not candidates for analysis—however much others may insist that they need psychotherapeutic help. All those who "need" an analysis are not necessarily analysable! No individuals, whatever their symptoms may be, are likely to draw much benefit from psychoanalysis or psychotherapy unless they fully accept that it is their wish to engage in this arduous, if fascinating, adventure. So our first requirement of future analysands is the recognition that they are anxious or depressed, disappointed or puzzled about themselves, have symptoms that do not make sense to them, or have discovered endless repetitions of the same unhappy experiences.

Personally, I would not accept in psychotherapy or psychoanalysis people who ask for analysis purely because they have been mandated by the courts or by a training institute, or because they have been encouraged by their doctors, their bosses, or their marriage partners to undergo this experience. To engage people in a therapeutic adventure solely on these grounds is to enter into complicity with a defense system of denial that might be virtually unshakeable. When potential patients seek help primarily because they make other people suffer or because others require them to do so, we may need several interviews to determine whether the individual in question is truly seeking self-knowledge. This brings us to the second important requirement of a future analysand.

2. The Search for Self-Knowledge

Going back to the first meeting between analyst and potential analysands, let us say that the latter do not plead for pills, nor are they there on someone else's behalf. This does not necessarily indicate a belief that their suffering arises from unknown factors in themselves. Many therapy seekers tend to blame society, family circumstances, their race, religion, heredity, or biological sex for their problems. The experience of psychoanalysis is not going to change these basic givens. While any of these factors may have contributed to current problems, if the individuals concerned do not seek to know *why* they continue to experience such unalterable factors in a traumatic way that renders their lives uncreative, they implicitly refuse responsibility for the direction of their lives. (The suffering of Kate related in Chapter 6 exemplifies this.)

The wish for further insight in order to discover the unconscious meaning of unsatisfactory life situations or incomprehensible symptoms implies acceptance of the fact that ultimately the causes of psychologiocal symptoms *lie within oneself*. This outlook is an indication that the potential analysand implicitly *accepts the concept of an unconscious mind*.

3. Is the Psychoanalytic Situation Bearable?

Of the many individuals who because of their suffering turn to analysts for help, a certain number are unable to use the psychoanalytic situation. This situation, in which one is called upon to "say everything" and at the same time "do nothing," is difficult for certain people to tolerate. When it seems unlikely that a patient will be able to accept this austerity and thus make use of the experience, it is up to the individual analyst to decide whether a modified form of psychotherapy, group therapy, psychodrama, or some form of psychiatric treatment may be more appropriate. Even when we judge that a potentially complicated patient (narcissistic, childlike, impulse-ridden, perverse, severely addicted, detached from reality, etc.) is able to withstand the painful aspects of the analytic relationship, we must ask whether *we* are willing to engage in the psychoanalytic adventure with this particular patient. Are we ready to tolerate the strain it will probably create in both partners, and to face the potential failure that such complex problems often entail? There is no denying that the going will be rough as we help certain patients towards a more creative way of living.

4. Can one Depend on Another without Fear?

One final factor to be weighed is the preparedness of the patient to *receive* help. Most would-be analysands project onto the analyst a certain omniscience, as though he or she already knows all that they do not know about themselves; however, some display a certain arrogance (usually born of fear) which suggests that they may be narcissistically wounded, rather than helped, by any discoveries they have not made themselves and may display a negative reaction to therapy. (This is illustrated by the patient Jack Horner quoted in Chapter 7.) Such narcissistic vulnerability may lay the basis for an interminable analytic experience.

In fact, every demand for freedom from psychological symptoms is a paradoxical one, in that these symptoms are childlike attempts at self-cure and were created as a solution to unbearable mental pain. There is, therefore, a strong internal force that fears the loss of symptoms in spite of the suffering they cause; this will tend to create considerable resistance to the analytic process.

Thus, on the basis of symptoms alone we have little insight into the direction an individual's analytic voyage will take. Many a so-called "good neurotic" may prove intractably unanalyzable while many a narcissistically fragile, borderline, or polysomatizing patient is capable of engaging in an exciting, creative and rewarding psychoanalytic experience.

The most "difficult" patients, those who cannot accept their share of responsibility for their symptoms or who cannot accept help because of their narcissistic frailty, may stir up painful countertransference feelings, since they make no apparent progress. They may even appear to get worse, feeling more unhappy, more hopeless, more angry than they were before they began their analytic voyage. For reasons unknown to themselves, they are terrified of the psychic change they seek and desire. This is understandable in that *symptoms are techniques for psychic survival*. It is not easy to let go of one's survival line when one has no confidence in the capacity for psychic change or a fear that all change will be for the worse!

WHAT THE PROGNOSIS FOR
PSYCHOSOMATIC ILLNESSES?

Severe psychosomatic afflictions, as well as the psychosomatic vulnerabilites that are part of everybody's potential problems, are often regarded as dubious areas for psychoanalytic investigation. When they do become evident in the course of an analysis, they are often ignored by the analyst as material for potential interpretation. In my early years of psychoanalytic practice I myself paid little heed to the body's incursions into the psychoanalytic process, but as time went by I was struck by the silence that shrouded psychosomatic distress — until it could no longer be denied. This "silence" became understandable to me as I began to realize that the roots of such phenomena were frequently found in early infancy.

On the basis of my early observations, I originally believed that in psychosomatic states the body was reacting to a psychological threat as though it were a physiological one; that there was a severe split between psyche and soma; that this was largely due to our somatizing patients' unawareness of their emotional states in threatening situations; that the ideas associated with conflictual affect were not repressed as in the neuroses but immediately wiped from consciousness (the mechanism Freud (1918) named *foreclosure* in connection with psychotic states). However, continuing observation showed me that many patients suffering from grave psychosomatic illness were neither operatory thinkers nor devoid of knowledge of their affective experiences (one such patient was Georgette, whose analytic process forms parts of Chapters 10 and 11). Clearly the earlier hypotheses were insufficient.

Studying the work of psychosomaticists dealing with the psychosomatic ills of babyhood enabled me to understand that my adult patients were at certain times functioning psychically like infants (from the Latin "infans" meaning one "who cannot speak"). Since babies cannot yet use words with which to think, they respond to emotional pain only psychosomatically. Although mothers think within the code of language (and most mothers talk constantly to their babies), the infant's earliest psychic structures

are built around nonverbal "signifiers" in which the body's functions and the erogenous zones play a predominant role. We are not
surprised when a baby who is suddenly separated from its mother
for a prolonged period of time or has been subjected to sudden
shock reacts with gastric hyperfunctioning or colitis. When an
adult constantly does the same thing in similar circumstances,
resulting in serious illness, then we are tempted to conclude that we
are dealing with an archaic form of mental functioning that does
not use language.

In addition, I came to realize that, since the infant has intense
somatic experiences in the earliest months of life, that is, long
before it has any clear representation of its *body image*, it can only
experience its own body and the mother's body as an indivisible
unit. Although infants seek interchange with their mothers and
early develop their own ways of relating to those around them, as
Stern's (1985) work has shown, they do not make well-defined self-
object distinctions.

When an adult unconsciously represents his/her body limits as
ill-defined or unseparated from others, emotional experiences with
a significant other (or sometimes anybody who happens fortui-
tously to mobilize the body's memory of early psychic trauma)
may result in psychosomatic explosion, as though in these circumstances there existed only one body for two people. The clinical
illustrations given throughout this book will clarify this notion
while throwing light upon my own psychoanalytic voyage into the
understanding of body-mind mysteries.

Before concluding this overture to the many theaters of the body
revealed on the psychoanalytic stage, let us consider one final
countertransference perspective. Manifestations of psychosomatic
phenomena often take us unawares, since patients frequently omit
mention of them. If and when they do become part of the patient's
analytical associations, they tend to reveal little or no language
links with underlying fantasy, such as we find with neurotic symptoms or with the neurotic sector of any given patient's psychic
structure. Moreover, many years may be required before the language links can be forged. For these reasons certain analysts tend
to take umbrage at somatic complaints. The fact that psycho-

somatic phenomena often escape the analyst's understanding, con-stitues a narcissistic affront and may lead certain analysts to feel that psychosomatic problems should be dealt with elsewhere, that our efforts should be confined to that which is psychological and capable of being expressed in words.

Added to these countertransference attitudes is the impression created by psychosomatic research publications stressing the un-availability of affect, the lack of imaginative capacity, and the difficulty in verbal communication. Admittedly, since its inception psychoanalysis, following Freud, has privileged the role of lan-guage in the structuring of the psyche and in psychoanalytic treat-ment. *But not all communications use language.* In attempting to attack any awareness of certain thoughts, fantasies or conflictual situations apt to stir up strong feelings of either a painful or an overexciting nature, a patient may, for example, produce a somatic explosion instead of a thought, a fantasy or a dream. (The psycho-somatic outburst of Christopher, related in Chapter 3, with its subsequent transformation into a dream and fantasies that could be *verbalized*, is a pertinent example.)

For these various reasons, as well as the fear that patients known to be subject to serious somatization may experience an exacerba-tion of their illness, it is understandable that some analysts do not welcome such patients.

However, if the preliminary precautions detailed in the preced-ing pages have been taken, there is no reason that a psychosomati-cally vulnerable patient and a caring therapist need refuse to set out together on the psychoanalytic journey. Even when the psy-chosoma threatens to disrupt or evade the work of analysis, the psychological rewards for both analysand and analyst may be con-siderable, as I hope to show in this book.

CHAPTER 1

Mater

My discovery that the body has a language of its own came when I was about five years old. From the time I was a child it had been the family custom, twice a year, to visit my Carrington grandparents, who had a large mixed farm in the South Island of New Zealand some distance from the city of Dunedin where we lived. There they raised crops and livestock of various kinds; they were particularly proud of their prize-winning Jersey cattle. My grandmother was a tiny, stern pioneer woman who looked and behaved for all the world like Queen Victoria. Her five sons and only daughter, as well as their spouses, always referred to her as "Mater." She ruled over "Pater," her dreamy artist-husband, as well as my Uncle Cedric and the numerous farmhands, just like an army colonel.

I disliked Mater intensely. She would not allow me to lie all day long on the verandah reading my picture books and making drawings. Instead I was to run around outside to get what she called "fresh air into my lungs" because I looked "so pale and citified."

12

My hostile feelings toward her were undoubtedly strengthened by the knowledge that, in the sanctuary of our home, my mother vociferated against the obsequious esteem paid to Mater by my father and his siblings. But I also knew that my mother was afraid of this imperious little Victorian woman and that she took pains as an English bride to appear to be a perfect daughter-in-law. In the same way she wished that I, New Zealander of a third generation, should be a model grandchild, but alas, within 48 hours of each biannual visit, I invariably produced a gigantic display of urticaria — a phenomenon that occurred only on the farm.

After some two or three years of this disgrace, it was commonly agreed by all members of the Carrington family that my urticaria was caused by the rich Jersey-cow milk that I loved to drink. This family theory was in no way demolished by the fact that the same Jersey milk, drunk elsewhere, did not produce the shameful bumps. Exasperated by anticipating once more the presentation of this less than perfect grandchild for Mater's exquisitely fault-finding eyes, my mother one day exclamed angrily, "We've had enough of these skin-bumps of yours! From the time we get to the farm you're not to drink one drop of milk!" Family legend has it that I replied, with the wisdom of a five-year old, "It's not the milk that gives me skin bumps — it's Mater!"

And indeed, subsequent events were to lend credence to my childhood theory that I was allergic to my grandmother! For when I was about eight, Uncle Cedric, who had carefully kept secret the fact that he was courting, suddenly annouced: "This is Edith. We're getting married this month." In no time, civil war broke out on the farm between Mater and her new daughter-in-law, with the result that my grandparents left to live in Napier — to my childhood mind the other end of the world — on the North Island of New Zealand. There they took up residence with Uncle Earnie, the only remaining bachelor among the sons, upon whom Mater could now impose her will. We continued to visit the farm, but less frequently, for without Mater nothing was quite the same — including the fact that I no longer suffered from urticaria! I could now drink the rich milk of Uncle Cedric's Jersey cows with impunity. Many decades have elapsed since that time and I have not suffered from that day to this from allergies of any kind.

However, I might add that from the time she left the farm, *Mater* began to perform on the psychosomatic stage. For the rest of her long life, she suffered from angina pectoris and for some 30 years her death was considered imminent. I remember thinking that God had punished her in the heart for being so bossy. But I must also have harbored a guilty fantasy that I was the cause of her cardiac pathology, for I prayed constantly to Him not to let her die of it! The miraculous response to my prayers did not, however, prevent my declaring at the age of 15, to the shock of my family, that I was an atheist and that I would see to it that my sister was inculcated in this new creed. No doubt my ambivalent feelings about Mater had now been transferred to God!

I still believe that both Mater and I myself were suffering from inexpressible grief and rage and that these contributed to our somatic manifestations. Meanwhile science had not waited for a child's fantasies regarding the origins of urticaria and cardiac pathology to develop theories to account for enigmatic somatic dysfunctioning.

A Theoretical Odyssey

In spite of my childhood pronouncements concerning the psychological causes of physical illness, in my first years of practice as a psychoanalyst I was not particularly sensitive to the manifestations of the soma on the psychoanalytic stage; nor was I preoccupied with the elusive body-mind relationship. I accepted Freud's implicit position that, although organic illnesses probably included hidden psychological elements, these were nevertheless outside the scope of psychoanalytic treatment and research. Freud's restriction of the psychoanalytic field to the psyche, in particular to its representational system as anchored through language, may seem surprising when one recalls that he firmly founded his whole theory of the psychic apparatus on biological territory and that he constantly drew attention both to the tendency of the human organism to function as a body-mind unit and to the fact that psy-

chic processess developed from biological ones. Despite his fascination with the interrelation between psyche and soma, he chose to
limit his research to the understanding of purely psychological
symptoms.

In the mid fifties and early sixties, like most of my colleagues at
that time (and many even today), I regarded the accounts of bodily
illnesses in the course of a session in the same way as I regarded
recountings of other everyday events. I listened to them as possible
displacements for preconscious or totally unconscious fantasy preoccupations. Therefore, apart from a self-query as to why my
analysand should think of physical states of health at this particular moment, I paid little heed to the potential nonverbal communication of which the somatic malady may well have been an external
sign.

My interest in the somatic self derived from a much wider field,
namely a preoccupation with everything that tends to *escape* the
psychoanalytic process — the multitude of important thoughts and
feelings that do not get discussed in sessions but instead are discharged in action outside the analytic relationship and its frame
and therefore elude understanding. All of us use action instead of
reflection when our usual defences against mental pain are over-
thrown. Instead of becoming aware that we are guilty, anxious, or
angry, we might overeat, overdrink, have a car accident or a quarrel with our neighbor or our life-partner or, weather permitting,
fall victim to the flu! These are simple examples of "expression in
action," through which one *disperses* emotion rather than thinking
about the precipitating event and the feelings connected to it. It
took me some time to observe in my patients that these forms of
discharge-in-action, where reflection would have been more appropriate, were a frequent cause of therapeutic stalemate and carried
the risk of an interminable analysis. The most elusive of these
phenomena appeared to me to be psychosomatic expressions, in
that the action took place in the patient's body and yet was clearly
not related to hysterical bodily symptoms. This led to much clinical and theoretical speculation on my part, and eventually to the
necessity for distinguishing between hysterical and psychosomatic
phenomena (McDougall, 1982a).

HYSTERICAL CONVERSION AND ITS CONFUSIONS

As I tried to understand more profoundly the *Studies on Hysteria* (Breuer and Freud, 1893–1895), I felt the need for greater theoretical clarity with regard to the clinical manifestations of bodily disturbance that could not be assumed to refer to an imaginary body with purely symbolic significance (as in the hysterias) and yet clearly displayed an hysterical dimension. In classical psychoanalytic theory hysterical symptoms refer to dysfunction when a body part or a sense organ takes on an unconscious symbolic meaning. For example, a patient's eyes or legs might be equated unconsciously with his or her sexual organs; in the case of massive inhibition of adult sexuality, an eye or a leg may appear not to function. There is no physiological damage; the affected organ is only hysterically paralyzed. But what are we to think of inhibitions of a more general order, such as sexual impotence and frigidity, or physical disturbances such as constipation, indigestion, insomnia and the like, in the absence of any organic illness? Here we find a confusing overlap between psychic and somatic phenomena. These dysfunctions cannot be entirely equated with hysterical paralysis or with the loss of vision or hearing in the absence of any discernible organic defect. While they may be classed today as hysterical-type manifestations, in that they result from unconscious anxieties about forbidden libidinal longings, they are also frequently found to be connected with aggressive and sadistic impulses and can with difficulty be comprehended as pure conversion of sexual wishes. Yet in all cases the mind is making use of the body in order to communicate something, to tell a story, and in so doing to prevent forbidden drives and wishes from being fulfilled. Before we can decide whether or not the surface symptoms refer to a classical neurotic structure we need to know something about the content of the repressed fantasies.

Let us suppose I have in analysis a patient who suffers from severe sexual impotence whenever he wants to make love. Once my patient's fantasy is brought to consciousness, we see that all women who interest him sexually unconsciously represent his mother. Immediately the woman in question becomes forbidden as an object of desire, and the men in the vicinity will be feared as potential castrators. It becomes understandable in these fantasied circumstances that he "needs" his impotence as a protective device. The patient, so to speak, castrates himself in advance. We might well consider such a symptom as an hysterical solution to neurotic conflict associated with the oedipal complex and its attendant castration anxiety. Neurotic fears are typically aroused when the normal adult right to pleasure in sexual and love relations or to narcissistic satisfaction in work and social relationships is unconsciously contested and therefore punishable.

Let us now suppose that another who suffers from the same symptom of severe sexual impotence eventually discovers that he is afraid he might lose the sense of his body limits while making love and "disappear" inside his partner, thereby "becoming" her and in consequence losing not only his sexual but also his individual identity. With such fantasies we leave the domain of neurotic anxiety to enter the more primitive territory of psychotic fears. Nevertheless, it should be emphasized that we find traces of these archaic fears in every individual's unconscious mind, for they are the fears – and wishes – of babyhood. (This point will be dealt with more fully in Chapter 2.) Such fears, associated with the infraverbal anxieties that arise in the mother-infant dyad, might be considered as prototypic of what later develops into the castration anxieties typical of the oedipal situation. The latter are marked by *verbal thought* as well as *a consolidated image of the body and its limits*. We might say that in the best of circumstances, the primitive longing for fusion, along with the terror this arouses for one's psychic survival as an individual, is partly dealt with by the oedipal crisis (along with the important role attributed to the father as a protection from this danger) and is therefore overtaken by the more sophisticated anxieties of this stage of maturation.

When psychotic anxiety as described above predominates in the clinical picture, it is doubtful that we are dealing with a classically hysterical structure; yet such patients cannot be considered psychotic. At most we might propose that many neurotic manifestations, both hysterical and obsessional, have an underlying psychotic core.

Nor can these intermediate forms of somatic perturbation be assimilated to well-recognized psychosomatic illnesses such as the famous "Chicago seven" (bronchial asthma, gastric ulcer, essential hypertension, rheumatoid arthritis, ulcerative colitis, neurodermatitis, thyrotoxicosis) first studied by Franz Alexander (1950; Alexander, French, and Pollock, 1968). These manifestations were originally considered (and are often so considered today) to be devoid of symbolic meaning. Alexander's research led him instead to posit certain specific personality organizations that appeared to correspond to well-delineated psychosomatic expressions.

THE ROLE OF THE MIND IN SOMATIC ILLNESS

In psychosomatic manifestations, the physical damage is real and the symptoms do not appear to reveal either a neurotic or a psychotic story (although they might ultimately acquire such significance, as I hope to demonstrate in succeeding chapters). The "meaning" is of a presymbolic order that circumvents the use of words. While psychotic thought may be conceived of as an inflated and delusional use of language, often used to fill spaces of terrifying nothingness (Montgrain, 1987), the thought processes of the psychosomatic sufferer frequently appear to have drained language of its emotional significance (McDougall, 1982a). In psychosomatic states the *body* appears to be behaving in a "delusional" fashion, often *overfunctioning* excessively (in contrast to the *inhibitions* of bodily functions discussed above) to a degree that appears physiologically senseless. One is tempted to say that the body has gone mad. This hidden similarity and at the same time striking difference between psychotic and psychosomatic organizations and manifestations has occupied my thought for some years. I have come to use the term "psychosomatosis" to indicate mental organizations in which the leading, or sometimes the only, visible reactions to disturbing fantasies and experiences are of a psychosomatic order.

As I began to observe more closely the somatic expressions of my patients in analysis, I came to the conclusion that psychosomatic phenomena could not, from a *psychoanalytic standpoint*, be

restricted purely to psychosomatic maladies, but should theoretically include everything that concerns the real body (not the imaginary body of hysterical conversion), as well physiological, including autonomous, functions. I therefore have come to consider as
related to psychosomatic phenomena all cases of physical damage
or ill health in which psychological factors play an important role.
These include accident-proneness or the lowering of the immunological shield when under stress so that one more readily falls
victim to infectious disease, as well as the problems of addiction,
which are a "psychosomatic" attempt to deal with distressful conflicts by temporarily blurring the awareness of their existence. The
ineffectiveness of this method of dealing with mental pain in any
permanent way accounts for the repetitiveness of addictive behavior. (The question of addictive solutions to emotional pain will be
more fully dealt with in Chapter 6.)

THE BODY AS THE PLAYTHING OF THE MIND

Although it is evident that anxiety is the mother of invention in
our psychic theater, the question of the symptoms "chosen" to deal
with it remains perennially open. Why does one person faced with
mental conflict create a neurotic response while another produces
a psychotic symptom and yet another creates a sexual perversion
or a psychosomatic malady? For example, when invaded by severe
anxiety about the wish to enjoy one's sexual life, one individual
constructs a neurotic symptom (such as premature ejaculation or
compulsive hand-washing), another develops a sexual perversion
that allows limited sexual expression, another creates a delusion
that his sexuality is influenced by washing machines, while yet
another, with no *manifest* sexual symptoms, develops, over the
years, skin allergies, asthma, tetany and peptic ulcers, all of which
may disappear when unrecognized sexual and narcissistic conflicts
are brought to light. (Such was the case with Isaac, quoted in
Theaters of the Mind, McDougall 1982a.)

The question of causality is further complicated by the fact that
it is necessary to distinguish between precipitating causes (such as
sexual arousal) and underlying causes, which may have their roots

in the earliest interactions between mother and infant and the early organization and structuring of the mind. Insofar as psychosomatic manifestations are concerned, it seems highly probable that certain ways of mental functioning predispose to a psychosomatic rather than a neurotic, psychotic or sexually deviant response to stress in identical circumstances.

Such speculations did not lead me immediately to a consideration of psychosomatic phenomena. Clinical observations first led me to reflect on the primitive significance of sexual deviations (McDougall, 1964, 1978) before coming to the conclusion that there was a more archaic form of sexuality, complete with pregenital, sadistic, and fusional aspects. This discovery led me to posit the concept of a psychosomatic *regression* to early, infantile erotism. I was still far from suspecting, however, that psychosomatic illness itself could be, in certain circumstances, the outward sign of extremely precocious libidinal longings (as in the case of Georgette quoted in Chapter 10) that were felt to be a threat to life itself. Nor did I imagine that, to express these findings, I would eventually coin a term like "archaic hysteria" (McDougall, 1982a) which may sound like a contradiction in terms since hysteria is constructed through verbal connections.

The Psychosoma on the Psychoanalytic Stage

As time went on I became more attentive to the psychic functioning of those of my analysands who, in addition to their psychological problems, suffered from allergies, heart and respiratory illnesses, gynecological disturbances, and other such maladies whose onset or reappearance appeared to be related to events of psychological importance to the individual concerned. I began to read widely on the psychosomatic aspects of these manifestations and to reflect at length on their psychological dimension insofar as I could observe this with my somatizing patients. Clinical observation slowly taught me that all analysands (and analysts as well) somatize at one time or another, particularly when stressful events override their usual ways of dealing with mental pain and conflict.

But those who most concerned me reacted to almost *every* situation that was emotionally arousing (particularly situations that mobilized anger or separation anxiety) with a tendency to fall ill. Frequently their maladies had been with them since childhood, although they usually did not think to mention these until thoughts about their physical health spontaneously arose in their associations. When I came to recognize the unconscious need, in a number of my patients, to *preserve* these illnesses, not only as a reassurance of one's bodily limits but also as proof of psychic survival, this was for me a notable discovery. With the passage of time I have made it a practice in initial encounters to invite future analysands to talk about their physical as well as their mental suffering.

A PSYCHOSOMATIC HEART?

Having discovered that two of my patients suffered from cardiopathology, I early on became interested in research work in this area (aided no doubt by my long years of trying to understand Mater or at least to deal with my conflictual image of her). I learned that reflection upon the psychological dimension of heart disease already had a long history. At the turn of the century, William Osler (1910) pointed out, in a treatise on angina pectoris, that these patients were in no way emotionally fragile or ostensibly neurotic. Osler's vivid portrait of the coronary heart disease patient has become a classically distinctive one. In the 1940s, the intensive pioneering research of Flanders Dunbar (1943) furthered the conviction that a specific personality pattern might indeed provide an etiological factor in the predisposition to cardiac pathology. Continuing research, particularly that of Friedman and Rosenman (1959; Rosenman et al.,1975), led to the now celebrated, although much criticized, concept of the "Type A personality." Friedman described this behavior pattern in the following terms: "A characteristic action-emotion complex which is exhibited by (coronary heart disease) patients who are engaged in a relatively chronic struggle to obtain an unlimited number of poorly defined things from their environment in the shortest period of time, and if necessary, against the opposing effects of other things or persons in the same environment" (Friedman and Rosenman, 1959). (Shades of Mater came back to my mind when I first read those lines.)

The fact that coronary heart disease occurred in epidemic proportions in the United States gave impetus to the devising of different methods for assessing the presence of what is referred to as the "coronary prone behavior pattern." Ongoing research appeared to demonstrate that the Type A personality pattern was as predictive of coronary disease as were factors such as high blood pressure, excessive cholesterol, or addictive tobacco smoking. Furthermore, a 1978 report from the American Heart Association indicated that patients demonstrating such a pattern were five times more likely to suffer from a second infarct than those who did not exhibit this kind of personality.

Psychoanalytic researchers, while inspired to further thought by such findings, are nevertheless more likely to direct their attention to uncovering the specific or leading ways of mental functioning and psychic structure associated with psychosomatic symptoms and in particular the extent to which these might be found to increase psychosomatic vulnerability. Before coming to a purely psychoanalytic approach to factors of causality, I would like first to turn to the findings of those who work in psychosomatic services.

The Research of the
Psychosomatic Specialists

Certain notable psychosomaticists with a psychoanalytic orientation have published research discoveries based on interviews with the many hundreds of patients seen in outpatient and inpatient services. Their work has given rise to two major concepts of mental functioning applicable to a supposed "psychosomatic personality." The first of these, *la pensée opératoire*, a characteristic form of operatory thinking, is a concept that evolved from the research of the so-called Paris School (Marty, de M'Uzan and David, 1963; Marty and de M'Uzan, 1963). Operatory thinking is marked by a pragmatic and affectless way of relating both to oneself and to other people, a form of relationship that appears to be largely delibidinized.

A patient of mine recounted in a preliminary interview that she had suffered since childhood from bronchial asthma. While the symptoms had receded with age, they would recur whenever she went to visit her mother; in fact, they would make their appearance as she began her voyage. When I asked her to tell me something about her mother, she said, "She's a big blousy-looking woman, quite handsome in her way, always busy with a thousand things. Of course, she's not as active as she used to be . . . she suffers from rheumatism these days." My patient was describing her mother as a stranger might have done—that is, from the outside. When I tried to find out what her feelings were from the *inside* about her relations with her mother, she became confused and said, "I don't really understand what you mean," as though she were out of contact with with her inner, psychic "reality."

A patient who had fallen gravely ill with ulcerative colitis was asked what events had occurred in her life just before the outbreak of her violent loss of bowel control. After some searching she recounted in a flat unemotional tone of voice that her parents and her fiancé had been killed in an autombile crash from which she had escaped unhurt. When asked what her reactions to this tragic event had been, she replied, "I just knew I'd have to pull myself together." A sensitive listener might read behind the spoken lines and understand that the young lady felt her whole life had been suddenly shattered and that much pulling together of the broken pieces would be required. She, however, had no conscious knowledge of such feelings and made no connection between the traumatizing event and her subsequent psychosomatic illness, in which her body exploded in an uncontrollable, life-threatening way.

Another patient who suffered a sudden outbreak of psoriasis that covered almost his entire body revealed that shortly before this he had run his automobile into a woman pushing her baby in a pram and had severely injured both. When asked what he felt at the time the accident occurred, he replied, "It was OK. I'm totally insured." Like the preceding patient this man saw no connection between his psychosomatic outburst and the accident. He seemed thoroughly "insured" against any knowledge of the overwhelming emotions that may well have been evoked in him momentarily at the realization that he had almost killed (perhaps even had unconsciously wished to kill) a mother and her baby. Instead, his body suffered a violent — and visible — reaction. Of course these apparently emotionless ways of reacting psychologically to serious life-events are not limited uniquely to psychosomatic sufferers. However, there is little doubt that a psychic economy which habitually treats potentially traumatic events with unusual calm and insensitivity, thus tending to eliminate any recognition of the overwhelming emotion that must undoubtedly have been mobilized, if only briefly, notably increases psychosomatic vulnerability.

The publications of the Paris school relating to the concept of operatory thinking gave rise to further research by psychosomaticists in Boston (Nemiah and Sifneos, 1970; Nemiah, 1978), who subsequently developed the concept of *alexithymia*. This refers to the discovery that certain people have no words to describe their emotional states, either because they are unaware of them or because they are incapable of distinguishing one emotion from another. They may not distinguish anxiety from depression, or excitement from fatigue, or indeed, anger from hunger.

My own interest in these apparently unemotional ways of thinking and experiencing and their contribution to psychosomatic vulnerability came about, as already mentioned, through my attempts to understand the many aspects of an individual's personality that escape the psychoanalytic process. Those of my analysands who seemed to refuse all knowledge of their psychic suffering, whether due to painful or exciting emotions (often *the feelings themselves* were felt to be forbidden or dangerous), appeared to pulverize their experiences, which therefore did not become available for thought. This also rendered any connection between the experience and subsequent somatic manifestations difficult to establish. The patients in question frequently claimed they felt empty, out of touch with people and events, much as though life were not worth living.

(Such was the case with Jack Horner, quoted in Chapter 7, and with Tim, whose analysis is discussed in Chapters 8 and 9.)

Analytic observation of these alexithymic and operatory reactions to psychological stress enabled me to see that these were frequently defensive measures against inexpressible pain and fears of a psychotic nature, such as the danger of losing one's sense of identity, of becoming mentally fragmented, perhaps of going mad. To this extent my slowly developing theoretical position differs from the theories of causality advanced by Nemiah and Sifneos, in that they see these as arising largely from neuroanatomical defects. While this may be the case for many patients who are seen in psychosomatic services, it did not apply to those I have worked with in analysis. Possibly we are dealing with two different populations, since analysands have come to analysis because of an awareness of psychological suffering while those sent to a psychosomatic specialist may be totally unaware of mental pain and unwilling to undergo any form of psychotherapy. In this case defensive structures against psychological exploration may be vitally necessary for their psychic equilibrium. (This mental state is illustrated by the patients discussed in Chapter 4.) An attempt to undermine these without the consent and cooperation of the patient may be potentially dangerous, perhaps even precipitating further somatic or psychological damage. The importance of detecting a neurotic dimension in a severely somatizing patient's psychic structure is one of the reasons for careful listening in initial interviews.

THE HEART OF THE MATTER

This leads me back to the question of heart disease and the extent to which cardiac vulnerability may be increased by the modes of mental functioning described above. Tim, whom we shall meet in Chapter 8, displayed a personality structure that closely resembled the portrait traced by the psychosomaticists. In the course of his analysis, he suffered a myocardial infarct. This tragic event led me (as well as Tim) to make several important discoveries which, while confirming some of the hypotheses of the psychosomaticists, also offered new insights into the unconscious dynamic significance of this kind of mental functioning. Over and beyond the psychic economy that is marked by operatory and alexithymic ways of relating to the world, we discovered early psychic trauma of a disturbing kind. In addition, this analytic fragment points to potential causes of such primitive forms of anxiety and perhaps illustrates the effects in adulthood of a preverbal child's early perception of affectless modes of functioning as a way of combatting psychological pain, early frustration and panic.

Recent research (Brazelton, 1982; Stern, 1985) provides ample evidence that infants constantly send out signals to their mothers regarding their wants and dislikes. Depending on her freedom from inner pressures, a mother will normally be in close communication with her infant over these signals. If internal distress and anxiety prevent her observing and interpreting her baby's cries, smiles, and gestures correctly, she may on the contrary do violence to the tiny communicator by imposing her own needs and wishes, thus plunging her infant into a continuously frustrating and rage-provoking experience. Such an eventuality runs the risk of impelling the baby to construct, with the means at its disposal, radical ways of protecting itself against overwhelming affect storms and subsequent exhaustion. The infant histories taken from adult psychosomatic sufferers frequently contain references of this kind to their infancy. Just as frequently, reports of very early autonomy (walking and talking at an unusually early age) add to the clinical picture.

NEUROTIC VERSUS PSYCHOSOMATIC SOLUTIONS

My first reflections on my clinical experience with somatizing patients had shown me that these analysands revealed few neurotic symptoms—to such an extent that I came to refer to them as "normopaths" (McDougall, 1978). It seemed they were obliged to maintain a camouflage of "pseudonormality" in order not to think or feel too deeply about inner pain and conflict that might otherwise be experienced as overwhelming and mentally disorganizing. Although many of these patients suffered from a variety of well-recognized psychosomatic maladies, they had rarely made any connection between their somatic manifestations and psychologically disturbing events in their lives, much as though perceptions of physical and psychological warning signals were totally ejected from consciousness. These perceptions were not denied or repressed and thus unconsciously registered, as occurs in neurotic psychic organizations. Instead all memory of the troubling perceptions was expelled or totally destroyed.

It was from analysands whose major methods of psychic defense were neurotic or characterological that I was able to learn most about this capacity to foreclose troubling perceptions from consciousness. Such a capacity for destroying meaning became analyzable when events that were strongly tinged affectively but not acknowledged resulted in temporary somatic manifestations or disturbed peceptual functioning. The excerpts from the analyses of Christopher (Chapter 3) and Jack Horner (Chapter 7) exemplify this specific form of psychological functioning, which results in what I have termed "psychic deprivation."

The seminal work of George Engel (1962) already advanced the theory that psychosomatic phenomena might be avoided in cases where neurotic organizations have arisen, in that the latter will perform a "buffering function" between mind and body. This means that the psyche that has managed to create a protective structure (in the form of a neurotic symptom) to deal with mental pain or psychic conflict may well be protected against somatic explosion. In psychosomatic afflictions there is instead a regression to more primitive forms of relationship between body and mind such as we may observe in psychosomatically disturbed infants. (See Chapters 4 and 5.) The same reasoning might be applied to addictive patterns as a way of dispelling mental suffering. (This will be discussed in greater detail in Chapter 6.)

This brings me back to the research of the psychosomaticists and their concepts based on extensive observation in psychosomatic services. Although their work has helped me to detect similar patterns of personality and psychic functioning in some of my patients (as in the already mentioned case of Tim), my work with analysands who somatized led me to question the psychosomaticists' theories as an adequate explanation of the cause of psychosomatic pathology (McDougall, 1982b, 1982c). I discovered that many severely somatizing patients — often suffering from multiple psychosomatic symptoms — did not display a pragmatic operatory way of relating either to themselves or to others, nor were they in any way alexithymic.

To the observations made in earlier writings (McDougall 1978,1982a), I would today add the following hypotheses:

1. Certain allergic, gastric, cardiac and other such reactions may be a somatic expression of an attempt to protect oneself against truly archaic libidinal and narcissistic longings that are felt to be life-endangering, much as a small infant might experience the threat of death.

2. To achieve this purpose, the psyche in moments of danger sends, as in infancy, a primitive psychic message of warning to the body which bypasses the use of language. Therefore, the danger cannot be thought about.

3. This may result in psychosomatic dysfunctioning, such as the urgent need to empty the body of its contents (as in ulcerative colitis), to hold one's breath (as in bronchial asthma), or to produce violent skin reactions (as in excema and urticaria). Alternatively, the psychic message might result in increased gastric secretion, heightened blood pressure, quickened pulse rate, and so on. Or again, the message may give rise to disturbances of such normal bodily functions as eating, sleeping, eliminating, etc.

4. The body, like the mind, is subject to the repetition compulsion. It may be recalled that in *Beyond the Pleasure Principle* Freud linked this manifestation to the destructive impulses. In the somatic sphere a complex body-mind reaction also tends to be inexorably repeated whenever the necessary stimulus (often of a visual, auditory or other perceptual-sensory nature) arises or when certain relationships with significant others are felt to be threatened.

5. The emotion aroused is not recognized in a symbolic way (that is, within the code of language which would have allowed the affect-laden representations to be named, thought

about and dealt with by the mind), but instead is immediately transmitted by the mind to the body, in a primitive nonverbal way such as flight-fight impulses, thus producing the physical disorganization that we call a psychosomatic symptom.

6. Psychosomatic maladies come to acquire, secondarily, a beneficial significance. The physical suffering they cause is liable to be compensated by the unconscious conviction that the illness is serving a protective function, such as defining one's body limits. Fears of merging when in affective interaction with others (recalling unconsciously a disturbed mother-infant relationship and the fear of being engulfed or abandoned by her) are thereby alleviated. Communicating a state of despair through organic illness may also give access to caretaking people. Analysis often uncovers one further fantasy, namely that the physically attacked body is at the same time a way of attacking the body of the internalized mother, thus providing a further secondary gain from illness.

7. In some cases physical illness may also be experienced as a reassuring proof that one's body is alive. The self is therefore reinforced against a feeling of inner death that stems from disturbed infancy. Such inner feelings frequently give rise to unacknowledged depression, since the individual takes this to be a normal mode of experience.

Readers may have already detected that several of the above statements could also apply, in varying degress, to psychotic symptoms. Despite the anguish hallucinations and delusions occasion, they are often felt to be preferable to the frightening nothingness of inner death that accompanies loss of one's sense of personal identity or bodily integrity. On the basis of these reflections I came to propose a certain similarity between psychosis and psychosomatosis, insofar as both states serve an underlying reparative aim in the face of an overwhelming, though often unrecognized, sense of danger (McDougall, 1982a, 1982b).

This brings me to the problem that has bothered me with regard to the use of language and its role — or rather its missing role in psychosomatic phenomena. The symbolic nature of hysterical and obsessional symptoms, which are created from once conscious, but subsequently repressed, verbal thoughts and connections, does not have a counterpart in psychosomatic symptoms. Nor is there a psychotic use of language and of words themselves, such as we observe with psychotic patients. In the latter words are intended less to communicate than to obliterate meaning (Montgrain, 1987; Ogden, 1980). Instead, with severely somatizing patients there is frequently a pseudonormal communication with the rest of the world (reminiscent of Winnicott's "false-self" concept, 1965), in which words, even language itself, tend to be divested of their emotional counterpart, at least in that sector of the personality that is constantly seeking to eliminate recognition of primitive anxieties with psychotic overtones.

Much later I was able to observe and conceive of an archaic form of symbolism in which the psyche was not bypassed, leaving the body "to talk in the mind's place"; rather, it was obeying messages that, while they did not pass through the language structures of the mind, were a stimulus to a somatic response, as in infancy.

The viewpoint that all psychological symptoms may be understood as infantile attempts to find a solution to emotional pain is easy to demonstrate with regard to neurotic and psychotic symptoms. However, this becomes difficult to accept when applied to psychosomatic illness. The above considerations all led me to postulate that, although many psychosomatic symptoms may rapidly lead to death (in contrast to hysterical bodily symptoms, which are purely symbolic and rarely cause physiological damage), paradoxically, they too represent an *attempt to survive*.

A lengthy vignette from the analysis of the polysomatizing patient quoted in Chapter 9 may clarify certain of these hypotheses concerning the psychic structure that lies behind many cases of psychosomatosis. This analytic fragment also gives insight into a personality pattern that differs widely from the personality profile drawn by the psychosomatic research workers. Since infancy and for some 40 years later this analysand had suffered from grave food allergies, neurodermatitis and bronchial asthma. As time went on, cardiac dysfunctioning, gastric ulcers and rheumatoid arthritis were added to these. These symptoms were slowly able to be given up by dint of painstaking analytic work on the part both of the patient and myself.

It is my hope that this and the other clinical illustrations to come may allow the reader to follow the extent to which the psychoanalytic experience is able slowly to transform the mute and mysterious messages contained in psychosomatic processes into verbalizable and therefore analysable psychoneurotic communications.

CHAPTER 2

The Body-Mind Matrix

Hᴏᴡ ᴅᴏᴇs ᴀɴ ɪɴғᴀɴᴛ acquire a sense of subjective identity? How does each of us become a "person," distinct from all other persons, in other words, an "individual" (a word which derives from the Latin "individuum," meaning "a unity that can no longer be divided")? Psychic life might be said to commence with an experience of merging, leading to the fantasy that there is only one body and one mind for two people, that they are one indivisible unity. Although already a separate being with innate gifts whose potentialities are as yet unwritten, the baby is unaware of this. To the infant, its mother and itself make up one whole person. Mother is not yet a distinct "object" for her nursling, but at the same time she is something much vaster than simply another human being. She is a total environment, a "mother universe," and the infant is but a small part of this immense and exciting unit.

Deeply buried within us all there is a longing to return to this illusory fusion, to become once again part of the omnipotent mother universe of early infancy, in which there is no frustration,

32

*merger vs individual
identity?*

no responsibility, and no desire. But in such a universe there is no individual identity either. We might even say that the fulfillment of such a longing would be the equivalent of the loss of personal identity, that is of *psychic death*.

AN INDIVIDUAL BEGINNING

The "one-body" fantasy has, of course, a biological prototype that originates in interuterine life, during which the mother's body must truly serve the vital needs of two beings. The prolongation of this experience as a wished-for state plays an essential role in the psychic life of the newborn baby. Everything that threatens the maintenance of this illusion causes infants to seek desperately to refind the lost interuterine paradise. In parallel fashion the baby's cries and signs of distress induce the mother to respond to this urgent demand and to seek, intuitively, *to recreate the illusion of oneness*, using the warmth, rhythm, and protective closeness of her body, as well as her voice. Through her capacity to maintain the illusion she enables her nursling to take in a vitally important *internal* image of the maternal environment, bringing comfort, or enabling it to fall peacefully to sleep.

Then there is the equally important need on the baby's part for separation. When a mother's recognition of her baby's need to differentiate is disturbed by unconscious conflicts that attack, for example, her infant's need to relinquish her physical presence in order to enter the world of sleep, this may precipitate one of the serious psychosomatic disorders of early infancy—the baby who suffers from insomnia and can sleep only while held in its mother's arms. The story of Sophie (Chapter 5) gives us a glimpse into this kind of mother-child relationship and its potential dangers.

When the mother-child relationship is "good enough," then from the early somatopsychic matrix will develop a progressive differentiation in the infant's psychic awareness, differentiation between its own body and that first representation of the external world that is the mother's body, the "breast universe." At the same time, that which is psychological becomes slowly differentiated in the infant's mind from that which is somatic.

This gradual "desomatization" of the psyche is nevertheless accompanied by the contrary psychic quest, to be completely merged with the mother universe. Babies will seek by all the means at their disposal, especially during moments of physical or psychological suffering, to recreate the illusion of bodily and mental unity with the magical breast universe, and at the same time will struggle just as fiercely to differentiate their bodies and beginning sense of self from the mother's body and self. As long as the mother's unconscious wishes do not lead her to interfere with this universal tendency of all infants towards both merging and differentiating, each baby, using the various psychological processes of internalization at the disposal of the psyche (incorporation, introjection and identification), will construct, first, an image of the maternal environment, and then, a mental representation of the mother herself as a soothing and caretaking figure, capable of containing her infant's affect storms and of modifying its suffering without thwarting its constant drive toward somatic and psychic autonomy. This will lay the groundwork for an eventual *identification*, in the infant's inner world, with the caretaking and comforting imago toward its own budding self.

THE BEGINNING
OF THE SYMBOLIC UNIVERSE

It is at this point in infant development that the baby begins to invent "security blankets" which, to the infant's mind, embody the essence of the mother's soothing and protective functions. The "pre-transitional" object (Gaddini, 1971,1975) may be one of the mother's garments, or a tiny piece of tissue that is impregnated with her odor and associated with the feel and warmth of her body. These highly invested objects, which allow the baby to sleep with the illusion of its mother's presence are in normal circumstances usually later replaced with more sophisticated mothering substitutes such as teddy bears or special rituals. (A breakdown in this process will be illustrated in the clinical vignettes quoted in the chapters to come.)

This is also the time when language begins to take over from the more primitive forms of bodily communication. The small child is

[handwritten marginalia: illusion of union is sweet if early experiences were not filled w/ anxiety ... aline ... word]

now able to think and pronounce the word "Mommy," thus creating the possibility of evoking her warmth and protection through
the word alone, without obligatorily requiring her reassuring external presence. This mental representation of "mother," as a person
who can be named and thought about, is essential to the structuring of the psyche and will eventually allow the infant to assure
for itself the introjected maternal functions, provided the word
"Mommy" represents a secure sense of comfort and safety.

As close bodily contact and gestural forms of communication
with the mother diminish, these are gradually replaced, through
the use of language, by symbolic communication. The infant becomes a verbal child. From this point on the contradictory wish to
be an individual while remaining an indissoluble part of the "other" is repressed; this longing is subsequently compensated by the
acquisition of an unwavering sense of individual identity.

However, the dream of potential access to the original and ineffable mother-child unity still claims its place in the unconscious. It
must be emphasized that the wish to rid oneself of one's essential
otherness, of both body and mind, in order to fuse with the primitive mother universe, persists in the heart of every human being.
But this nostalgic yearning does not necessarily lead to a *pathological* outcome. To allow oneself to drift, physically and psychically,
towards the illusory realization of this desire contributes to, among
other manifestations, the accomplishment of two essential human
experiences, both psychosomatic *par excellence*: the enjoyment of
sleep and the pleasure of orgasm. Likewise, either of these human
experiences may become disturbed if the fantasy of fusion with the
mother universe is impregnated with anxiety. This may arise from
the fear of a void or the terror of a death-dealing imago, where
there should be an introjected maternal object with soothing qualities. Either of these dangerous images would lead to the irrevocable loss of oneself, rather than the triumph of the life-giving image
illuminated by the illusion of an erotic and mystical union.

ONE BODY, ONE SEX, ONE MIND FOR TWO

For many years I have sought in my analytic work to "hear" this
muted quest for a fusional union when it is accompanied by the

terror of losing the sense of one's bodily and individual self. I have
been able to trace its fantasied extensions as follows: one body for
two, one sex for two, one mind for two, finally, one life for two.
The conceptualization of these primitive modes of mental functioning, as well as the defensive network constructed from early
childhood to deal with their inherent danger, present a number of
theoretical difficulties. The most important of these is that our
classical psychoanalytic models of mental functioning, to the extent that they are based on *meaning*, are insufficient for conceptualization of the manner in which psychic life is organized from the
period before the infant becomes a verbal child, and well as inadequate to explain the way in which psyche and soma are slowly
differentiated from each other while remaining forever linked.

My first experience with the fantasy of "one mind for two"
occurred in working with severely disturbed children (McDougall
and Lebovici, 1960). This was extended later in clinical work with
analysands suffering from narcissistic vulnerabilities. These patients taught me that they had difficulty in distinguishing between
my mind and theirs, a problem that also had repercussions in the
outside world. Frequently, these analysands were convinced that
their thoughts about what was occurring in my mind were absolute
certitudes. In the same way they often made an implicit demand to
be understood without having to resort to speech — a demand legit-
imate on the part of the nonverbal nursling, but apt to create
stressful misunderstandings in adult relationships.

Later, in clinical work with homosexual patients (McDougall,
1964, 1978), and those I referred to as "neosexual" patients (Mc-
Dougall, 1982a, 1986), I came to appreciate the force of the unconscious fantasy of "one sex for two." These deviant sexual choices
sought to create a protection not only against conscious fears concerning sexual rights and sexual identity feeling (that is, all that is
included in the psychoanalytic concept of "castration anxiety"),
but also against unconscious anxiety over losing one's sense of
individual identity (which might be thought of as a prototypic
form of castration anxiety). Through the imaginary possession of
the sex of the partner, there is invariably revealed a fantasied recovery of one's own sexual integrity which keeps castration anxiety at

bay while at the same time protecting from the more primitive fear of the loss of body limits or of the sense of personal identity.

With regard to the fantasy of "one body for two," the importance of this way of relating to another person was brought home to me through attempts, over the years, to understand the economic and dynamic significance of recurrent psychosomatic phenomena in the course of the analyses of a number of my patients. Their fundamental fantasy often ran as follows: "Love leads to psychic death, that is, to the loss not only of my mental barriers against implosion from others but also of my body limits. Nothing short of total indifference towards any loving attachments can assure my survival." It then becomes necessary to maintain a barrier of "disaffectation" toward others, that is, a barrier created by the loss of all awareness of affect (as exemplified in Chapter 6), and even toward the narcissistic investment of one's own body and mind. This in turn may, to an alarming degree, increase psychosomatic vulnerability, becoming a threat to life itself, as many psychosomatic researchers have observed in the well-known clinical phenomena of "alexithymia" and "operatory thinking" referred to in Chapter 1. (The story of Tim, recounted in Chapters 8 and 9, illustrates this kind of psychic organization but advances a conception of the disaffected state that differs from that described in psychosomatic research.)

An area of inner deadness that tends to infiltrate the psychic reality of such patients often leads to a lack of physical self-care and an unawareness of emotional pain (or even excitement and pleasure), to the point that there is a regressive resomatization of the ejected affective experience and, in some cases, the lowering of immunological barriers.

However, it must be emphasized that many alexithymic and operatory-thinking people do *not* fall somatically ill, and others who suffer from a number of serious psychosomatic maladies do *not* display the operatory and alexithymic character shell that typifies the psychosomatic patients who have been the most studied in psychoanalytic research and in psychosomatic services. On the contrary, in my psychoanalytic practice I have had a number of polysomatizing patients who were intensely aware of their affective experiences.

Sometimes the "dead area" of despair that so often inhabits these analysands is masked by an addictive dependence on significant others, who are experienced as part of themselves. Any perturbation in relation to these vital others is apt to plunge the patient into overwhelming anguish, accompanied by a recrudescence of the psychosomatic symptoms. In the analytic situation such phenomena tend to reappear in response to every separation from the analyst, thus offering the possibility of putting into words, for the first time in the patient's history, the primitive nonverbal signals that are being relayed by the mind and lived out through the body. (This is clearly exemplified in the vignette given in Chapter 10.) Unacknowledged representations, charged with affects of terror and rage, are also frequent elements in the precipitation of psychosomatic phenomena.

It must be reiterated that the path to individuation (which, when it is fully integrated, acts as a potential barrier against severe psychosomatic or psychotic breakdown) is tortuous and full of hazards for every child. At the same time, it is evident that some part of every individual's identity will forever be linked to what he represents for another, for subjective identity, as Lichtenstein (1961) pointed out, is always determined by two dimensions: "that which resembles me" and "that which is different from me." All people who belonged originally to the external world, who have been significant from birth onward, become stable mental representations that form an intrinsic if unconscious part of the internal psychic world. Although the manner in which this occurs still remains mysterious, this should not prevent us from attempting to answer the questions that arise from the complicated psychic event called internalization. The following queries come to mind:

- How does an infant come to acquire a representation of its own body and become aware that this *body* is uniquely his or hers? And what are the consequences should this psychic possession fail to be truly established?
- How does one's *sexual identity* become a secure psychic representation and what allows for the acquisition of the conviction that one's genital is also a unique possession (with the

conviction that is does not belong, for example, to one's parents)?
- And what of the *mind* itself? How does the child come to understand that its mind is a treasure trove of which he or she alone is the owner, with full rights over the thoughts, feelings, and intimate secrets that it encloses?

During the century since Freud's initial conceptualization of the oedipal organization, this concept in its phallic-genital version has become considerably enriched both theoretically and clinically. We have acquired much insight into the conflicts, at different stages of the oedipal organization, that give rise to neuroses and to perversions. We have also garnered extensive information regarding the representation of the body, the sexual organs and the mind as they are invested in neurotic and perverse organizations. With the psychoanalytic models we possess we are able to demonstrate the way in which neurotic and perverse organizations come into being as a reaction to what children have been told — or not told — about sexual identity and sexual roles. From there we can trace the way in which the child who still lives on within the adult has attempted, throughout childhood, to interpret incoherent communications stemming from the parents' unconscious wishes and fears.

But we know notably less about the early structuring of these representations, the preoedipal infrastructures that lie behind, for example, psychotic and psychosomatic organizations. Consequently, we also possess less insight into the psychotic and psychosomatic vulnerabilities of every human being. Although Winnicott, Bion, and other post-Kleinian research workers have made invaluable clinical and theoretical advances into the archaic foundations of the human psyche, the metapsychologies of psychosis and of psychosomatosis have yet to be written. But of one thing we can be certain — psychotic and psychosomatic manifestations, like neuroses, character problems and perversions, are also attempts at self-cure. These constructions are the psychic work of a small child faced with mental pain that arose from external factors beyond its control.

With regard to early infancy we must remember that a baby's

earliest external reality is its mother's unconscious (in large part structured by her own childhood experiences and beliefs), in that this governs the quality of her presence and her ways of relating to her nursling. Almost as powerful a factor is her relationship to her baby's father and the extent to which he is invested by her with both real and symbolic significance and affection. This leads us to consider the presymbolic, preverbal universe as possibly providing a key to psychotic and psychosomatic potentialities.

Thus, our understanding of psychotic and psychosomatic phenomena requires models of mental functioning that help us to conceptualize the way in which psychic life is structured from its very beginnings, in a presymbolic universe in which the mother plays the role of her infant's thinking apparatus. Infants are notoriously avid to discover and control the sources of pleasure as well as to avoid experiences of suffering. A nursling learns very quickly to distinguish between those gestures and movements that bring its mother closer and those which are met with no response or even induce rejection. In recent years research into mother-nursling interactions all tend to demonstrate that "communications" between baby and mother may break down very early in the relationship, due perhaps to sensitivity on the part of certain infants, but also due to the mother's varying ability to understand and interpret her baby's needs and primitive communication of these. She may sometimes be led, because of her own inner problems, to impose with undue force her idea of what she wants her baby to feel or need rather than trying to interpret the messages the baby is sending forth. In the same way, catastrophic *external* events, such as sudden death of an important person in the mother's or father's world, socioeconomic strife, war or holocaust experiences, frequently play a pernicious role. In such cases, much depends on the parents' presence and capacity to contain and soothe both their own and their children's distress. With regard to psychotic and psychosomatic manifestations in adults we may detect, in the course of analysis, primitive defense mechanisms that are within the scope of tiny infants, the infant part of the person being encapsulated within the adult personality but always ready to take over the psychic scene when circumstances become unduly stressful.

THE EARLY DEVELOPMENT OF MIND

Many psychoanalytic researchers have formulated concepts to describe the early organization of the psyche from birth onwards, and even to trace its development from the prenatal period. All are attempting to conceptualize the ways in which infants interact with the objects of their external environment and thus come eventually to take psychic possession of their bodies, their sexual identities, and their minds. Evocative metaphors characterize different aspects of these psychic processes, such as Bion's (1962, 1963) "transformation of beta elements into alpha functioning," Lacan's (1966) "manque à être," Klein's (1935) concept of the "paranoid-schizoid" and "depressive" positions, Mahler's phase of "symbiosis" and of "separation-individuation" (Mahler, Bergman, and Pine, 1975), Winnicott's (1971) concept of "transitional space," Kohut's (1971, 1977) "self-object" concept, Stern's (1985) concept of a preverbal "awareness" and the sense of an "emergent" and a "core self," Ogden's (1988) concept of an "autistic-contiguous" position, etc.

All these authors acknowledge, either implicitly or explicitly, the fact that experiences of separation and the recognition of existential differences are the poles around which the sense of self and of individual identity is constructed. Whenever separation and difference are not experienced as psychic acquisitions that enrich and give meaning to instinctual life, they become *feared* as realities that threaten to diminish the self-image or to empty the individual of what is believed to be vital for psychic survival, namely the maintenance of the illusion of fusional oneness with the archaic mother-image of babyhood.

Most of the analytic authors mentioned above would also agree that in order to attain a firmly established sense of self an infant needs a relationship with a mother who fulfills her maternal functions not only of acting as a protective shield *against* overwhelming stimuli from without but also of decoding sensitively her infant's communications to her and its recurrent need *for* stimulation.

The slowly acquired psychic representation of the mother is intimately linked with her capacity to modify her baby's physical or psychological pain. A baby that is hungry, wet, hurt, frightened, or angry can do nothing about these states except by producing fleeting moments of hallucinatory satisfaction. With the slow introjection of the mothering environment, the infant will begin to distinguish between itself and its mother and look confidently to the mother to bring comfort and relief from physical or mental suffering. When, however, a mother fails to shield her infant from traumatic overstimulation or exposes it to equally traumatic understimulation (particularly when it is in a state of distress), this may well lead to an inability to distinguish between the self-representation and the representation of the other. This in turn may give rise to an archaic body representation, in which body limits, the investment of erogenous zones, and the distinction between the mother's and the baby's body remain confused.

In discussing the problems of projection as related to the failure to maintain the protective shield, Freud, in *Beyond the Pleasure Principle*, wrote that

towards the outside it [the psychic apparatus] is shielded against stimuli, and the amounts of excitation impinging upon it have only a reduced effect. Towards the inside there can be no such shield. . . . First, the feelings of pleasure and unpleasure (which are an index to what is happening in the interior of the apparatus) predominate over all external stimuli. And secondly, a particular way is adopted of dealing with any internal excitations which produce too great an increase of unpleasure: there is a tendency to treat them as though they were acting, not from the inside, but from the outside, so that it may be possible to bring the shield against stimuli into operation as a means of defence against them. This is the origin of *projection*, which is destined to play such a large part in the causation of pathological processes. (p. 29)

Thus, we may understand the way in which certain somatizing patients who have been exposed to continuing trauma in infancy (in that external stimuli became so powerful that they broke through the protective shield), tend to attribute their ills to outside circumstances, since primitive emotional states have failed to achieve a mental elaboration of a symbolic or verbal kind.

When separation and difference are feared as experiences that may destroy the sense of self, and the subject feels impelled to struggle against the primordial division that gives rise to an "individual," this may result in a variety of psychic "solutions": sexualization of the conflict; the construction of narcissistic or borderline personality patterns; addictive solutions such as drug or medicament dependency, alcoholism, or bulimia; or a profound split between psyche and soma. The latter offers two different kinds of solution. The first leads to autistic pathology, in which case the body and its somatic functioning frequently remain intact while the mind closes itself to the external world; the second keeps the relation to external reality intact, with the risk that the soma will begin to act in what we might call an "autistic" fashion, that is, detached from the psyche's affective messages in terms of word-presentations, leaving powerful thing-presentations to seek non-verbal expression.

Thus, in later life, psychic pain and mental conflict arising from inner or outer stress are not recognized at the level of verbal thought and discharged through psychic expressions such as dreaming, day-dreaming, thinking, or other forms of mental activity; rather, they may lead to psychotic solutions of an hallucinatory kind or find discharge in psychosomatic manifestations, as in early infancy. In psychoanalytic practice we are frequently faced with somatic dramas that are the signs of inaccessible—that is to say inexpressible—psychological dramas, for the body, like the mind, is subjected to its own form of repetition compulsion. Thus, these signs contain psychic messages that escape mental representation. How are we to "listen" to them? And how eventually may we hope to render them symbolic and thus communicable through language?

There is one further complication in the analysis of patients who somatize extensively. Sooner or later we discover that our analysands fiercely *resist* the search for the psychic factors that nourish psychosomatic vulnerability. They fight, as do our neurotic and psychotic patients, with a determination of which they are unaware, to *protect* their somatic creations. It would even be foolhardy to push certain patients to examine these mental factors if their resistance to this were very strong or the wish to know more about their causes totally absent. However, a number of psychosomatically vulnerable analysands experience the analytic frame and the relationship with the analyst as comprising a safe place where they may explore their hidden, primitive fantasies and the profoundly archaic scenarios of their inner theater. In these fortunate circumstances we may then discover that psychosomatic manifestations have a psychological history that is capable of reconstruction. I shall now summarize briefly my earlier reflections on these matters, since they have been stepping-stones to my present view of psychosomatic phenomena in the psychosomatic process.

A Brief Review of Earlier Observations

In former writings (McDougall, 1978, 1982a) I attempted to single out certain elements that were usually present in those of my analysands who demonstrated a strong tendency to somatization. In summary, I came to the following conclusions:

1. The missing link between the hysterias and psychosomatic states may be found in Freud's (1898, 1914, 1916–1917) concept of the "actual neuroses."
2. This missing link is closely connected with the metapsychology of affect. Freud (1915a, 1915b) designated three possible "transformations" of emotion (conversion hysteria, obsessional neurosis, actual neurosis). It seemed to me possible to add a fourth transformation in which, following the model of the psychic foreclosure of mental representations, an affect could be stifled in its expression, without any compensation for the loss of the experience or its recall (McDougall, 1982a). That is to say, the foreclosure from consciousness would be compensated neither by the formation of neurotic symptoms nor by the recovery of foreclosed ideas in the form of delusions, as described by Freud in, for example, the case of Schreber (1911a). In such instances we might posit that the psyche is in a state of deprivation. This hypothesis will be dealt with more fully in the following chapter.
3. The majority of these analysands appear to have attained a

normal oedipal organization and are able to lead sexual and
social lives of a normal, adult kind. However, the analytic
process tends to reveal, with certain exceptions, that this oedipal structure has been grafted onto a much more primitive
organization, in which the paternal imago appears damaged
or even totally absent from the patient's inner psychic world.
The father's sex and presence seem to have played little role in
the mother's life; therefore he frequently appears as a person
whom it is forbidden to love and who is unworthy of esteem.

4. As a consequence, the image of the internal mother becomes
   extremely dangerous. When there is no fantasy of the father's
   penis playing a libidinally and narcissistically enhancing role
   in the mother's life, the mental representation of the mother's
   sex (which she transmits to her child) becomes that of a limit-
   less void. The child runs the risk of projecting into this void
   all the offshoots of infantile megalomania, without encoun-
   tering any obstacle. The fantasy of the mother's inner space
   then appears constantly enticing yet at the same time terrifying.

5. A further consequence of this fantasy structure is that the
   father's phallus, detached from its symbolic psychic role, becomes split in two: on the one hand, an idealized penis out of
   reach of the child's capacity either to desire or identify with;
   on the other, a destructive and persecutory part object of an
   omnipotent kind.

6. The mother's image, as well as the fantasy of her body, is
   also double: an idealized representation offering the eternal
   promise of ineffable bliss, and a part object that threatens
   psychic or even physical death.

7. This introjective family constellation, unbalanced and anxi-
   ety-arousing, reflects the unconscious conflicts and contra-
   dictions of the parents themselves. This seems on many occasions to have prompted the children to very early autonomy,
   as a consequence of their prematurely regarding the parents
   as *distinct and separate objects*. When, for example, the
   mother has not been introjected into her infant's psychic
   world as an "environment" or inner state composed of sooth-

ing and protective functions, but instead is *precociously apprehended as a total and separate object* (Ogden 1986), this mental image becomes charged with omnipotent and ideal qualities that are out of reach. This is accompanied by the installation of an unduly early form of autonomy, which leaves the child and adolescent-to-be with feelings of total inadequacy. The infant has a vital need to maintain the illusion of being one with the mother for a considerable period of time, so that the mother-baby image only gradually is differentiated into a mother and a child. It is this illusory fusion that allows small children to sleep and to digest and eliminate their food — in other words, to function somatically without disturbance, convinced that the mother universe will take care of everything.

8. One further consequence of the above disturbance is a disruption of the normal transitional phenomena of infancy, as described by Winnicott (1951). This potential transitional space begins to be constructed during the first year of life, allowing the infant slowly to create an inner psychic space; that is, the baby begins to internalize the first traces of maternal functions, with which, for brief moments, it can identify, until it reaches the stage of maturation in which it achieves the "capacity to be alone in the presence of the mother" (Winnicott, 1965). In the relationship described by Winnicott as "primary maternal preoccupation," typifying the relation of the mother to her newborn babe, a part of the mother is also merged with her nursling, so that in a sense she shares the infant's illusion. This in turn permits her baby to experience the relationship in the same way. However, certain mothers experience their babies as small foreign bodies, different from themselves. These infants feel deprived and often display early psychosomatic reactions. Other mothers cannot *themselves* bear to relinquish the fusional relationship, thus setting the stage for allergic ailments or serious eating and sleep disturbances (as in the case of Sophie quoted in Chapter 5). In either event, the infant establishes the vitally necessary feeling of separate identity only with considerable difficulty.

This then hinders the little child in taking psychic possession of its body, its emotions and its capacity to think or to link thoughts and feelings. One further consequence may be an attack on the capacity to enjoy intersubjective relatedness (Stern, 1985).

This leads us inevitably to take account of the mother's unconscious, as reflected in the child's mental representation of her. This emerges slowly in the course of an adult psychoanalytic treatment. Long before the acquisition of language, gestures, movements, and the free expression of emotional states may be experienced by the infant as forbidden. Aulagnier (1975, 1984) has emphasized the importance of such interdictions in those who become psychotic. The growing child understands that it is forbidden to *think*—the only permitted thoughts are the mother's, so that the child must eventually invent its own vision of the world in order to escape the terror of being entrapped in the mother's mind. In those who are in no way psychotic but instead suffer from grave psychosomatic illnesses, it has been my experience that certain highly charged emotional thoughts, which the mother cannot bear, become totally forbidden or foreclosed thoughts for her child. (This is exemplified in Chapters 8 and 9.)

In the same way, certain bodily zones and certain physiological functions may not be contemplated or must be rendered devoid of pleasure because of the manner in which they are invested by the mother. For example, a patient who suffered from gastric ulcers and many neurodermatological maladies "discovered" during the course of his analysis that he "possessed" for the first time in his life his anus and its functions (McDougall, 1978). The disavowal of certain bodily parts or functions, like the foreclosure of affect-laden ideas, is undertaken by the small child in order to prevent a tearing apart of the indissoluble mother-baby link. In fantasy, either the child or the mother will fall apart or be torn to fragments if this does not take place. The mother's image is again double: that of an omnipotent and omnipresent figure, and that of a woman who is frail and easily broken. (The case illustration in Chapter 10 gives vivid insight into the compelling force of such fantasies.)

When a representation of fusion between the two bodies of infant and mother persists, this leads either to almost total denial of the significance of others or else to panic in the face of every evidence of separateness and otherness. If the lack of identification with an internal caretaking mother figure continues, this often gives rise to the conviction that one is not responsible for one's bodily well-being. The fantasy of not truly possessing one's own body or (which often amounts to the same thing) the unconscious fantasy that one's body is under the control of another also plays an important role. Thus, somatic expressions tend to arise in place of unrecognized psychotic fears and wishes.

Failure in the fundamental process of becoming an individual will inevitably compromise the infant's capacity to integrate and recognize as personal possessions not only its body and its erogenous zones, but also its mind, that is, its thoughts and feelings. When inadequate elaboration and discharge of psychological tension through psychic work or action are joined to an inability for self-care, we find that these patients simply ignore the body's signs of suffering and fail to hear the mind's distress signals. In such cases the resulting split between psyche and soma may have catastrophic consequences.

One aim of this book is to study, from a psychoanalytic viewpoint, the unconscious significance of psychosomatic manifestations and to examine the extent to which these are linked to the vicissitudes involved in becoming a person and to failures of the internalization processes by which individual identity is constructed. The theoretical questions, which shall be explored further in the chapters to follow, have been urged upon me by my clinical experience with analytic treatments that seemed to founder because conflict and psychic pain that should have been verbalized were instead being expressed largely through somatic discharge.

From the point of view of clinical theory, important first questions emerge: What is the relationship of psychosomatic phenomena to the symptomatology of neurosis and psychosis? When there is little sign of neurotic symptom formation or of psychotic recovery of lost parts of psychic experience through the creation of a neo-reality, can we envision that the mind may be genuinely *de-*

prived of some experience which once formed part of it? Can we establish that such deprivation leaves the body open to decoding and carrying into action primitive signals from the mind? Consideration of these questions will form the major part of the next chapter.

CHAPTER 3

On Psychic Deprivation

Cᴀɴ ᴛʜᴇ ᴘsʏᴄʜᴇ ᴛʀᴜʟʏ ʙᴇ "deprived" of some element that once belonged to it? Psychoanalytic theory uses concepts such as repression, denial, disavowal and projection to describe the manifold ways in which bygone thoughts, feelings, memories, and fantasies have *disappeared* from consciousness. Yet these are not lost. They are still capable of recall under special circumstances or may find their way into our dreams, slips of the tongue, slips of memory, and sudden unaccountable fantasies; they may find expression in repetitive experiences, inhibitions, symptoms, and sublimations. These varied psychological events indicate that the psyche is never genuinely deprived of the thoughts, perceptions, sensations, or events that it has once experienced, even if, at a later time, these appear to be beyond conscious recall.

We are all unaware, much of the time, of what is occurring in our psychic reality. This is particularly evident in the unusual stories we create in the altered state of psychic awareness called dreaming, as well as in psychological symptoms of which we tend

50

to feel ashamed because they, like our dreams, often seem strange and illogical. In particular, those who undertake psychoanalysis come to discover that they have been conscious of only a small fraction of what composes their inner psychic world. As Freud, in his paper on "Contructions in Analysis" put it, the work of analysis "resembles to a great extent an archeologist's excavation of some dwelling-place that has been destroyed and buried . . . [but] the analyst works under better conditions and has more material at his command to assist him, since what he is dealing with is not something destroyed but something that is still alive " (p. 259).

The fact that our psyche functions, dynamically and economically, in ways of which we are unconscious, does not mean that the psyche is deprived. Few of us, for example, are conscious of our infantile sexual longings, with their inevitable procession of incestuous, homosexual, and pregenital themes. In the same vein, we are all relatively unconscious of childhood mortifications, with their quota of infantile rage, or of the envious and often murderous feelings that the child hidden within us still entertains towards those who were nearest and dearest to us in childhood. These primitive impulses all have a number of potential outlets in adult life. Ideally, our narcissistic, aggressive, and early libidinal strivings will find adequate expression in our sexual and love relationships and in our professional and social lives, as well as in so-called sublimated activities. Thus, when our primitive emotional states of mind are adequately invested and find expression in these different ways, all that lies behind our everyday experience is repressed from conscious memory.

However, when desires that are conflictual, forbidden, or impossible are only partially compensated or are suddenly blocked in their felicitous expression and subsequently find no adequate outlet, then repressed fears and longings may again come to the surface. When this occurs, they tend to give rise to neurotic symptoms or inhibitions that keep the troubling conflictual wishes from consciousness, thus permitting the individual to continue with his daily life. But this is only achieved by paying the tribute of mental suffering. The same may be said of psychotic symptoms, which frequently represent a delusional compensation for what has been

ejected from consciousness. Neurotic and psychotic symptom formations therefore take the place of what has been excluded, so that
once again our psyche is not deprived—it has been compensated.

In spite of the individual solutions each of us has achieved in
order to maintain psychic equilibrium, everyday life still provides
many occasions for stirring up forbidden or frightening ideas.
These may take the form of troubling thoughts, fantasies, or sensations that intrude upon the mind, or they may be nothing more
than simple perceptions—the sight of a poster in the street, a flash
of lightning, a sudden crash, an overheard conversation, or an
unusual word—capable of mobilizing conflictual or painful mental representations. Nevertheless, we are usually able to put such
psychic assaults "out of our minds" for the time being, sometimes
so rapidly that we no longer remember them. They then become
the potential furniture of dreams or perhaps the nodal points for
artistic and intellectual creations. Or they may simply find discharge in daydreams. Whatever their fate, we are again compensated for what has been lost from consciousness. It should be emphasized that if we lacked this capacity to remove from consciousness
troubling thoughts and perceptions, the continuity of our psychic
lives in their conscious dimension would be constantly threatened.
We would be bombarded with unwelcome anxiety or overstimulat-
ing wishes and therefore unable to go about our everyday lives.
(This predicament occurs in the altered states of consciousness
manifested, for example, in psychotic breakdowns or while under
the influence of drugs.)

However, it may happen that, because of certain ways of mental
functioning, the emotional impact of the external world (due to
fleeting perceptions, traumatic events, conflictual relationships
with significant others, or personal events such as births, deaths,
or marriages) is excluded not only from consciousness, but also
from the symbolic chain of meaningful psychic representations.
The experience therefore goes *uncompensated*. In the same vein,
the pressure of the internal world of instinctual demands—libidinal, sexual, and narcissistic deprivations, envy, rage, or continually unacknowledged aggression, and so on—may also fail to achieve
mental representation. Thus these demands can be neither re-

pressed nor subsequently used to form neurotic or delusional symptoms or character pathology.

When the psyche, either temporarily or in a quasi-continual manner, is unable to recover what has been excluded from consciousness through symptom formation, discharge in dreams, or in some other form of psychic activity, the mind may perhaps be described as in a *state of deprivation*. There is a void with which the psyche will try to deal, but its messages will be primitive and the mental functioning that results will tend to produce a reaction of a somato-psychic order, as in infancy. A child's immaturity and incapacity to use verbal thought render impossible the use of more complex ways of dealing with overwhelming affect storms and unmanageable excitement or mental pain. We see, therefore, that at this stage of existence what the psyche is truly deprived of are *words*, or more specifically, what Freud called word-presentations (1915b). Instead the psyche has access only to what he referred to as thing-presentations. These thing-presentations are dynamically powerful, unconscious elements expressed in the form of a perceptual or somatic registration of emotional arousal, which must then be decoded by the psyche and subsequently carried into action. This is precisely what happens when we are the victims of psychosomatic manifestations; a regression to infantile ways of psychic functioning is taking place. In other words, a short-circuit in the use of language and secondary process thinking has occurred. These regressive pathways are open to all of us throughout our lives, so that we are all capable of "somatizing" our emotional distress when external or internal pressures overwhelm our normal ways of thinking upon and reacting to situations that cause mental pain.

PSYCHIC REPRESSION VERSUS SOMATIC EXPRESSION

The practice of analysis offers frequent occasions for observing the somatic consequences of psychic deprivation. This is particularly revealing when it occurs with analysands who in general are not inclined to somatization as their predominant response to stressful circumstances and the mental pain to which they give rise.

When clinical experience has allowed me to discover some of the underlying primitive roots and the preverbal significance of sudden psychosomatic events, this has led me to consider these somatic explosions as an archaic form of hysteria, in contrast to neurotic hysteria which, as classically defined, is predominantly dependent on language links and seeks to deal with anxiety concerning one's adult *right to sexual and narcissistic gratifications*. The substitute symptoms that the psyche creates are intended to take the place of, or act as a punishment for, libidinal wishes, whether these are invested in external objects or in the narcissistic self-image. The level of conflict that I am conceptualizing in using the term "archaic hysteria" with reference to psychosomatic phenomena is concerned more with protecting one's *right to exist* than with guarding one's right to the normal satisfactions of adulthood. Here we are dealing with the anxieties that are aroused when the sense of individual identity, or life itself, is felt to be threatened with extinction. As already emphasized in the previous chapter, the libidinal strivings of an infant may be thought of as vacillating between a wish for fusion with the mother-body and a wish for complete independence. Provided the mother's unconscious fears and wishes or the pressures of external circumstances do not render her incapable of modifying her infant's physical and psychological suffering, she will enable her baby to maintain, in times of physical or mental pain, the illusion of being one with her. When the infant is impeded in its attempt slowly to create an internal representation of a caring and soothing maternal environment and to identify with this "internal" mother, the lack of an internal protective figure persists into adult life. (The psychosomatic disturbance that gives rise to life-threatening infant insomnia is one manifestation of this lack in babyhood. The story of Sophie recounted in Chapter 5 exemplifies this.)

Somatic dysfunctioning in repsonse to stress of any kind might well be thought of as a symptom through which, as with classical hysterical symptoms, the psyche seeks to send messages that are interpreted somatically. The means are, however, more primitive than in hysteria. Thus, in psychosomatic states, a body organ or somatic function might be perturbed for no organic reason, yet act as though it were called upon to take psychological action in a biologically threatening situation. For example, an individual's body might act as though it were trying to "get rid of" something poisonous (as in ulcerative colitis in which the body contents are brutally ejected), or as though it were trying to "hold onto" something (as in bronchial asthma, in which the patient frequently cannot expel his breath). Why would the bowel continue to empty its contents in the absence of any organic pathology? And why would anyone hold his breath, in fact almost stop breathing, without a physical reason for doing so?

Such somatic phenomena arise in response to messages from the psyche, as it attempts to deal with what are dimly perceived as threatening experiences; nevertheless, the individual concerned is frequently unaware of this aspect. Paradoxically, although the psychosomatic reaction is intended to protect the individual from psychological damage, it may in fact endanger his life. In archaic hysteria therefore, these phenomena do have a psychological meaning but of a presymbolic order, in that they are the result of a primitive attempt to deal with what we might well term psychotic anxieties, were they to be consciously recognized and believed to be imminent. But neither psychotic nor neurotic symptoms have been created to compensate for what has been ejected from consciousness, because the anxieties aroused have been unable to achieve a mental representation in a symbolic, verbal (i.e., thinkable) form.

The Unwanted Child

I shall illustrate some of the above ideas with a vignette drawn from the analysis of a man who was not a gravely somatizing patient. Nevertheless, he appeared to lack any trace of a maternal caretaking figure with whom to identify in his inner universe, and could thus be thought of, according to my hypotheses, as potentially vulnerable to either temporary psychotic or psychosomatic incidents. This analytic fragment also demonstrates the possible relationship between psychosomatic phenomena and breakdown in dream functioning.

Christopher was a 40-year-old psychiatrist, married with two children. He and his wife, also a psychiatrist, were both reasonably successful and well-regarded in their careers. Christopher had already been in treatment for ten years with a well-known male psychoanalyst. "It was a typically Lacanian analysis. X . . . was almost totally silent throughout those years, but I tried hard to give him what I felt he wanted and did profound research into the signifying elements of my mental structure. My professional work improved considerably. Before that I was a mediocre student with little confidence in my ability to follow my chosen path." He then added, in a despairing tone of voice, "But my analysis was entirely an intellectual adventure. I'm still as ill at ease in my physical and my mental self as I was before I began — as though I don't really inhabit my own body nor my own self."

Christopher's symptoms, as well as his memories, all pointed to an extremely perturbed mother-child relationship. To begin with, Christopher, an only child, had been told all his life that he was unwanted and that his conception had obliged his parents to get married. He remembered that as a little boy he was always terrified of getting lost and that he would stick closely to his mother "in order to find his limits." He recalled vividly his fear when she went to the bathroom and locked the door behind her. He would hammer on the door, crying, frightened that he might begin to feel "lost" in her absence. According to his mother, everyone had believed, until Christopher was about 12, that he was somewhat backward mentally — until an uncle, of whom he was very fond, declared that even if Christopher whispered rather than speaking out, and tended to hide himself away from others, he was a highly intelligent little boy. Also in his twelfth year Christopher fell ill with pulmonary tuberculosis — a serious somatization to which reference will be made later. At this time he spent a year in a sanatorium where he developed both physically and mentally into an alert and active youngster. According to Christopher, the separation from his parents had been highly salutary.

The First Interview

In addition to the biographical details given above, and the brief account of his earlier analysis, Christopher explained that he sought analytic help at the present time because of the suicide of a woman patient whom he had been treating for severe delusional states. This woman, married with three children, brought about her death by setting fire to herself during her psychiatrist's recent vacation. Christopher had been very attached to this patient, had kept many notes on the progress of her therapy and had discussed her case extensively in group supervision with an analyst experienced in the psychoanalysis of psychotic patients. In addition to a feeling of narcissistic mortification in the face of his colleagues, he also felt extremely guilty, as though this tragedy were due to some irresponsibility on his part. He wondered whether his patient's unexpected and fatal act was linked to his own state of perpetual anxiety.

In both his professional and private life, Christopher felt "inadequate," "confused," "perplexed" with regard to the right course of action to take in many everyday circumstances. He claimed he was consequently overdependent on his wife, continually on the lookout for her judgments, seeking her approbation and fearing her disapproval. The theme of "loss" recurred incessantly. Christopher would become "lost" in his thoughts, as well as in his projects and his work. In the course of the analysis, his identity papers, his briefcase, his camera equipment, and his keys were regularly displaced and, as often as not, irretrievably lost. During his initial interview with me he recounted some of these facts in a muffled and sad tone of voice, like a man who had also lost all hope of being able to enjoy life. The suicide of his patient, now also lost to him, had reinforced his feeling of inadequacy in all areas of his life.

With regard to his physical self, Christopher mentioned in passing two symptoms with psychosomatic overtones. He talked of an irritable bowel condition for which no organic cause had been detected, but this was a rather intermittent occurrence and troubled him little. He was more concerned about his frequent insom-

nia, since he often had difficulty in falling asleep and would sometimes wake up feeling anxious but with no memory of any dreams.

My overall impression was that Chrisopher seemed to have little
insight into his state of depression and narcissistic depletion. In
addition, he paid little heed to his childhood experiences and the
relationship with a mother whom he had nevertheless presented in
a rather cruel light.

It is not my intention to give a full account of this lengthy
analysis (in which the psychosomatic elements did not play a major role), but simply to illustrate a certain type of mental functioning which in my opinion increases psychosomatic vulnerability
(among other possible symptomatic outcomes). Such mental structures appear to become organized in early childhood, when the
mother-child relationship has *failed* to give rise to an internal representation with caretaking functions (with which the child needs
eventually to identify if he is to aquire the capacity for both physical and mental self-care). The image of the mother in these cases
tends to be split. On the one hand, there is an idealized, inaccessible, and omnipotent mother-image, potentially able to take away
all suffering and satisfy every wish; however, this plays a persecutory role in that the child can neither deserve nor attain this grandi-
ose ideal. On the other hand, there is a rejecting and death-bearing
image of the mother with whom the child, once he has become an
adult, will identify, consequently behaving in similar manner to his
own child-self. When, in addition, the father appears to have
played a rather muted role in the child's life, being therefore represented in his inner world as someone indifferent to his child's well-
being, such patients act as shockingly careless parents towards
themselves. They tend to look either to the world of others or to
addictive substances to repair their sense of damage. These combined factors contribute to a disturbed sense of subjective identity
with a concomitant lack of distinction between self and object.
This favors the persistence of unrecognized psychotic anxieties
regarding one's bodily and psychic integrity and eventually facili-
tates psychosomatic expressions.

Before coming to a dramatic somatization that occurred during
the analysis, I should like to mention briefly the somatic event

mentioned by Christopher during his first interview—the sudden onset of pulmonary tuberculosis when he was 12 years old. This period of his life had given rise to many memories and associations among which we discovered certain psychological factors that may have contributed to Christopher's falling ill at this specific time. All his childhood memories led him to believe that he was an extremely sad and withdrawn little boy. He linked this to his conviction that his mother did not love him. Consequently he turned to his father in search of support for his narcissistic self-image. Shortly before the appearance of the tuberculosis, his father not only had suffered a serious setback in his professional activity but had also had a grave physical accident. Christopher remembered seeing his father bleeding, and his concern that he might die. The knowledge that his father had lost his employment redoubled his anxiety. We came to the conclusion that these events, which coincided with the stresses of puberty, may have greatly exacerbated Christopher's already existing depression and increased his vulnerability to infection.

A Somatic Drama on the Psychoanalytic Stage

The analytic fragment which follows is drawn from two consecutive sessions in the fifth year of Christopher's analysis with me. I had taken these notes, as I frequently do, following a vacation break.

CHRISTOPHER Our vacation wasn't too great . . . because of the new boat. I couldn't seem to control it . . . and most of the time I couldn't even get it started. Then I also spent a terrible night which left a searing impression on me. I'd been asleep about an hour and I suddenly woke up in great pain. My whole abdomen was monstrously swollen. I had fantastic diarrhea and explosions of stomach gas that lasted for hours. It was something spectacular. And the pain was atrocious. Even after I had the pain under control with medication I couldn't get back to sleep for the rest of the night. In fact, the diarrhea is still going on. Truly I don't understand what happened to me that night.

Over the years I have learned to treat somatic events of this order, when recounted in a session, as "communications" of a mute or infraverbal kind with an underlying significance of both a dynamic and an economic order. I approach them much as I would the account of a dream, searching, for example, for some glimpse into day residues. I asked Christopher, therefore, whether anything in particular had occurred the day before his terrible night.

c Well . . . yes . . . all day I'd struggled with the boat . . . impossible to get it started. After about two hours my wife said, "What we need is a *man* to help us!" At the time I agreed fully, yet now I come to think of it, her remark was quite shattering. Talk about being castrated! And on top of that she had gone on again about wanting a third child. I still feel threatened by this . . . it's too much . . . too soon. I can't face it.

JM It seems you hadn't "digested" your wife's remarks very well that night. Do you think that your body, instead of your mind, was reacting to all that had happened in the day?

(There followed a long pause.)

c Perhaps I was trying to make a baby for her . . . that monstrous swelling . . . and it was something like giving birth.

Although I did not say this to Christopher, I thought to myself that, if his interpretation were accurate, his somatic staging of the pregnancy theme resembled an abortion rather than a birth. Then I also wondered, in view of the material from previous sessions, whether Christopher's interpretation of his somatic illness expressed unconscious envy of the woman's capacity to bear and to give birth to children. If this hypothesis were correct, then Christopher would seem to be expelling such unconscious wishes, giving to the incident an hysteric overtone.

At the following session Christopher recounted a dream.

c Last night I had a horrible nightmare. I had a newborn baby in my hands and I was getting ready to roast it. I put it on a spit and watched over the cooking carefully, without a trace of concern or guilt. Then I began to eat it, starting with its hand.

And I offered its arm to someone, maybe my wife. At that
moment I became suddenly aware of the tiny stump of an arm
and I began to feel afraid. The thought came to me in the
dream, "My God, you've committed a crime! It's forbidden to
eat children. When he grows up he'll be crippled. I've damaged
him for life." I was flooded by a feeling of horror and my
mounting panic woke me up in the middle of the night. I was
sweating and trembling and couldn't get back to sleep again for
thinking about the dream.

The similarity and at the same time dissimilarity of the nightmare and the nightmarish vacation experience recounted at the
preceding session immediately captured my attention. But not
Christopher's. His first association was to a dream that his *psychotic patient had made* shortly before her suicide. She dreamed
that she took her youngest child (the third) and boiled it until there
was nothing left "but its little heart beating in her hand." In the
dream she rushed to her psychiatrist for help, asking him to make
the child whole again.

In listening to Christopher's associations the following thoughts
went through my mind: First, Christopher had frequently referred
to this woman's ambivalence toward her youngest child; his inability to understand this particular dream, in which she specifically
appealed to him for help, had also left him feeling ill at ease when
it was first recounted. At one point I had said, because of the
context in which he had recalled his patient's dream as well as his
continuing determination to understand it, that we could imagine
that the "little heart that continued to beat" perhaps also represented the patient's own childlike heart. Now it seemed to me that the
same fantasy might apply to the eaten arm of the baby in Christopher's dream. Perhaps the infant Christopher had become "a
cripple for life." Was not he the crippled child, incapable of secur-
ing his mother's love and equally incapable of managing a boat
and thus gaining the esteem of his wife? Perhaps he was offering
his arm (a gift of castration) to his mother or wife as a survival
technique?

But was there not also an underlying fantasy that his own greedy aggression might be responsible for his woes? For we find on this particular dream stage Christopher-the-cannibal who eats other people's babies. Possibly he projected onto his mother his own damaging oral love. Christopher was an only child and no doubt unwanted, as his mother claimed, but these very facts made him fearful that another might arrive who would be more worthy of her love. He had once said he felt "burned" by his relationship to his mother since she seemed perpetually unloving and out of reach. Was he getting rid of these imagined babies by eating them, burning them or "boiling them up"? (Clearly, the patient's dream of boiling her baby had made as lasting and perhaps as traumatic an impact on her psychiatrist as the horror of learning later that she had deliberately burned herself to death. It is not surprising that he subsequently found himself unable to use the dream and to further his patient's insight into her own deep conflict.)

Christopher felt he had been a "bad mother" to his patient and in his own dream he is no doubt identified not only with the damaged child but also with the terrifying mother. The dream-script reads: "Look, mothers cook and eat their babies." His association to the psychosomatic explosion recounted at the previous session seemed to read: "Mothers wish to abort their babies." To what extent was he identifying with a "killer-mother"? Christopher's earlier dreams and fantasies concerning women and their pregnancies led me to feel that one potential interpretation might be directed toward the fantasies of getting rid of unwanted children and another to his envious feelings towards women coupled with the fear of identifying with the woman as a baby-murderer. In addition, Christopher's firm refusal of his wife's request for another child seemed to follow the same pattern. I limited myself to the remark that "not all children are wanted."

This intervention led Christopher to connect the dream theme, for the first time in this session, with his wife's insistent demand for a new baby. Then he added that she had actually brought the subject up once more the preceding night.

c But I can't bear to think I made this dream. The very thought makes me feel ill.

Indeed, thoughts of this order, if excluded from consciousness, might well have contributed to Christopher's digestive illness during the vacation, particularly since they had not found expression in a dream or in some other form of mental activity. We might also propose that, when a frightening fantasy cannot find expression through a dream, this suggests that the psyche does not have access to the words required for this particular fantasy. Words are remarkable containers of feeling and may prevent highly charged emotional experiences from seeking immediate discharge through the soma or release in action.

c I'm as psychotic as my patient. I understand now why she committed suicide! I feel such hatred for myself. I can't tolerate this dream.

JM There are two people speaking at once in you at this moment — the adult who treats himself as psychotic and hateful, a child murderer, and the infant who tries to communicate his distress through this dream. This is a child terrified that others may come and take his place and he will then feel "damaged for life." He must eat up any others that threaten his existence. Your wife's insistent demand for another baby is perhaps as threatening as would have been your mother's wish for another baby. You become once more the small frightened child you have so often told me about. The adult in you can't tolerate this distressed child, doesn't want to listen to him, and may even want to kill this helpless, monstrous baby-self.

c The unwanted child! Yes, *I* don't want him either!

JM The killer-mother?

c That's what I was to my patient, an incapable, murderous mother. And we were both killer-mothers in our dreams!

I then reminded Christopher that at our last session he had recounted a quarrel, during the vacation with his wife, that had been followed by "monstrous" diarrhea and a night of insomnia. This time there is no somatic explosion but an explosive dream that was also followed by insomnia. This proved to be an important turning point in Christopher's elaboration of his relationship to

the anxious child-self whose messages he had tried to stifle for so
many years. It also heralded the possibility of analyzing his ambivalent love-hate feelings toward, and homosexual envy of, women.
These themes occupied many succeeding sessions and brought
many new associations into Christopher's psychoanalytic discourse.

From the material contained in this short vignette I would make
the following hypotheses: The events of the day preceding Christopher's massive gastric perturbations had mobilized in him extremely primitive fantasies which had never been put into words
and which would have evoked affects connected with distress, rage,
envy, and oral sadism. But Christopher was totally unaware of this
archaic dimension. I would suggest that my patient's body had
reacted as though it had been poisoned because he was deprived of
the knowledge of wordless fears and the primitive fantasies that
were just becoming capable of verbalization.

The horrifying themes expressed in the dream are closer to psychotic fantasies than the fears associated with neurotic organizations. But in Christopher's case the foreclosure from the psyche of
certain important mental representations, accompanied by the loss
of the associated affects, was not recovered by delusional formations, as in the psychoses. Instead, a radical split between body
and mind had occurred. Messages sent by the psyche were not
transmitted through the symbolic chains of verbal thought and
word-presentations; rather, short-circuiting the links of language,
they were registered only as *thing-presentations*, provoking a direct
somatic response, such as we observe in small infants. The persistence of this kind of mental functioning, reveals frequently, in the
course of analysis, its roots in the early mother-child relationship.
The mother's unconscious problems or stressful circumstances
may prevent her from providing a sheltering space in which her
small child can develop a more mature form of psychic organization when in the throes of primitive emotional states. Innate
vulnerabilites, such as neurological impairment or cognitive disor-
der, may also hamper the *infant's* ability to take in and process the
mother's empathic response. Whatever the cause, there has not
been a "good enough" mother-child relationship.

This deduction in Christopher's case is supported by his other psychosomatic complaint—his severe insomnia. Lewin's research (1946, 1948) led him to propose that manifest dreams are like a technicolor motion picture projected onto a blank screen that is the dream representative of the breast, and that "blank dreams" represent the refinding of the early breast relationship. If these hypotheses are accurate, then one might question the capacity of certain patients, who have had a perturbed mother-child relationship, to fall asleep with ease and "regress" to the blank-screen state. If the breast-mother was experienced as unreliable or incoherent in her relationship to her nursling, this might impede the ability to dream at all. Thus the normal discharge that unconscious conflict, highly charged with emotion, seeks through fantasies and dreams is often lacking. (I have found similar disturbing representations of the mother in a number of analysands suffering from insomnia. These patients frequently seemed to behave like Ferenczi's "wise babies" (1931). In a sense the "babies" must be parents to their own nursling selves. Incapable of reliving the primary fusion with a supportive maternal introject, they must stay awake so that no harm comes them.)

Christopher's constant fear of separateness and loss, coupled with his difficulties in sleeping, led me to the assumption that, for obscure reasons, his mother had failed to ensure the basic maternal function of shielding against overwhelming stimuli both from within and from without. The sleeping tablets he took constantly no doubt played the role of a transitional object, since he appeared to lack an inner maternal object capable of permitting him to fall safely asleep. As Winnicott (1951) pointed out, experiences of overstimulation consequent upon the mother's failure to provide a screening function, if often repeated, will contribute to the creation of a "false self." In Christopher's case this took the form of pseudo-deficiency in his intellectual functioning and, later, of character defenses against the psychotic anxieties with which he was constantly threatened. These served to mask a persecutory representation of his mother, while keeping at bay considerable depressive affect associated with infantile rage and oral aggressive fantasies.

I would propose that, when affective links are stifled, this rift between psyche and soma may concomitantly favor a break in the links between primary and secondary processes. Some patients actually come to discover — and this was true in Christopher's case — that they have always believed it was forbidden, even dangerous, to function mentally, and that mental elaboration of affect-laden situations should therefore be avoided to the utmost. Due to a breakdown in dream functioning, there is no adequate discharge of tension through hallucinatory dream formations, nor does the psychic structure lead to psychotic manifestations. Instead, one tends to observe disturbed somatic manifestations. The psyche is, as it were, impelled regressively to utilize preverbal and archaic body-mind ways of expression. The messages signaled by the psyche are of the 'fight or flight' order, but these receive no further elaboration than they would in the mind of a small infant under the sway of primitive instinctual tensions. Thus, only the physiological root of the affect is discharged. The psyche has done what it can without words.

When we are able to give expression to primitive feelings and fantasies through our dreams (where we are all permitted to be deluded and hallucinated) and through freedom to daydream, it is possible that these may prevent the body from acting in a "delusional" way, that is, reacting with somatic responses that obey no biological need. In Chapter 8 we shall have the occasion to follow the analytic adventure of a man who, when he first came to analysis, claimed that throughout his life he had never known what it was to have a dream.

As for Christopher, it is interesting to hypothesize that perhaps he felt the need to be back in the analytic relationship before allowing himself to make his frightening nightmare. Through my absence on vacation, I too no doubt joined the cohort of "killer-mothers" in his internal world.

Whether my interpretations were accurate or not (perhaps other interpretations of his underlying fantasies would have worked as well) and whether my theoretical conceptions will stand the test of time or not, my patient's attacks of colitis ceased. As he became progressively more tolerant of his wild child-self and better able to parent this distressed child, he ceased identifying with the rejecting internal mother. He also began to allow the creation of dreams that more adequately fulfilled their function, so that the severity of his insomnia decreased. Little by little he ceased to react like a "burned baby," became less lost in his everyday life, and actually began to look forward to creating a third baby with his wife, since he no longer needed to keep this place for himself.

CHAPTER 4

The Psychosomatic Couple: Mother and Child

ONE LIFE FOR TWO?

T HIS CHAPTER ATTEMPTS no more than a thumbnail sketch of a certain kind of mother-child relationship that appears intimately connected with serious somatization. My encounter with the two patients of whom I write occurred within a relatively short space of time. Each suffered from the same serious illness and in both cases its outbreak or exacerbation appeared to be closely linked to the relationship each woman maintained to her only child. It will be seen that the vignettes display the same initial unwillingness, on the part of these distressed mothers, to consider that this illness may have a psychological dimension. The interviews also reveal the difficulty—and perhaps the inadvisability—of engaging such patients in psychotherapy. The two encounters made a lasting impression on me and aroused in my mind a number of tentative hypotheses, which had to await further clinical experience for some degree of confirmation.

68

Mrs. A came to see me at the insistence of a specialist in gastroenterology. Her doctor, whom I did not know, had read some of my published work dealing with psychosomatic phenomena in a psychoanalytic situation. His referral letter stated that Mrs. A had in the last three years suffered two severe attacks of ulcerative colitis, the second necessitating surgical intervention. A slim, elegantly dressed woman, Mrs. A sat with legs crossed, looking very composed. Our conversation went something like this:

MRS. A My doctor said I must come to see you since you're a psychoanalyst.

JM Would you have come to see a psychoanalyst otherwise?

MRS. A Well . . . no! I'm saner than most people I know. But my doctor says ulcerative colitis is psychological.

JM What do you think? Does it seem to you that you have many psychological problems?

MRS. A Well, I have great faith in my surgeon. And as he pointed out, the second attack nearly cost me my life. Yet I can't see what my problems really are.

Having drawn a blank with my initial gambit, I invited her to talk about the attacks and the conditions under which they had occurred.

MRS. A The first was three years ago. I was terribly overworked getting my new business going, never a moment to myself. But I love my work. It isn't a source of problems for me.
(Silence.)

JM Were there any important events other than your new business?

MRS. A Well . . . er . . . it was just after my daughter left home to continue her studies in Paris.

JM How did you feel about her leaving home?
(Silence.)

MRS. A Oh, she was so keen to get her post-doctoral training. (long pause) My daughter is the center of my life. Until she left home she *was* my life.

JM You must have felt bad about her leaving?

MRS. A Oh no! I would never have stopped her.

Sensing Mrs. A's resistance to going further into this question
through her slight misrepresentation of my query (for she replied
as though I had asked, "Didn't you want to stop her?"), I attempted to create an encouraging space in which she might feel
safe to explore her feelings about losing "the center of her life" —
perhaps a feeling that life itself were being drained away from her.

JM It's understandable that you wanted your daughter to continue
    with her studies, but still you may have felt rather sad after she
    had gone?
MRS. A It's normal for children to pursue their studies.

Not wishing to be intrusive into what could well have been inexpressible pain, I then suggested that Mrs. A tell me about the
second attack of ulcerative colitis, in which she had "almost lost
her life." ("Had her daughter become even more lost to her?" was
my unspoken question.)

MRS. A The second attack? Let's see . . . oh yes! The business was
    growing fast, getting more and more complicated and I felt I
    needed help. I just can't manage alone.
JM Did anything else of importance occur around this time?
MRS. A Let's see . . . yes, it was just after my daughter got mar-
    ried.
JM How did you feel about that?
MRS. A I was very pleased, naturally. After all children do grow up
    and get married. She'd only known him a few weeks when they
    got married, but it seems she'd met the right man.
JM You like her husband?
MRS. A Oh, I hardly know him. He's a Yugoslav. They live in
    Belgrade. I never get to see her anymore.

I thought to myself that Mrs. A's daughter had put considerable
distance between her mother and herself and wondered whether
her mother's unconscious demands upon her to be her "life" had

proved difficult to bear. I limited myself to remarking that her daughter was nevertheless a very important person in her life. She proclaimed this to be normal since mothers are always attached to their children, but followed this up with the remark that she had stayed 25 years in an unhappy marriage solely for her daughter's sake. She had never been truly in love with her husband, but her parents were in favor of the marriage; although he was a hard worker, her husband earned less than she did, was a hearty drinker, and had always been more interested in his male friends than his family.

Mrs. A had no difficulty describing the irritating aspects of her marital relations. In contrast, she seemed quite unable to elaborate upon on her emotions regarding her relationship to her daughter, her daughter's decision to study in Paris, or her sudden marriage two years later. She eliminated any reference to personal feelings in the face of these two successive departures, each of which had been followed by an outbreak of ulcerative colitis. It seemed she made no connection between her illness and her separation from her daughter and referred, in this context, only to her all-consuming business affairs. The implication appeared to be that she had no time to worry about anything else, as though she left no space for feelings of sadness or anger over the loss of this daughter for whom, nevertheless, she felt she had sacrificed 25 years of her life as a woman.

I told her what, in fact, she had already told me—that although she filled her days with hard work, her daughter's marriage and emigration to a far-off country had resulted in the loss of someone very dear to her, particularly since she felt deprived of a loving relationship with her husband. I added that this could be an emotionally painful situation. She gazed at me as though trying to seize the meaning of what I was telling her, and then added, as though it were a shameful admission, that she "had a need to feel loved and wanted."

A long silence followed.

MRS. A May I discuss a very important *personal* question with you?

JM By all means.

MRS. A Well, I needed help with my business. I opened two other
    branches and this man applied to be my assistant—he's very
    young but so keen and intelligent. I'm thinking of taking him
    into partnership.

With considerable difficulty she then told me that he had fallen
deeply in love with her, and she with him. For the first time in her
life she was engaged in a passionate relationship with a man. She
felt tempted to leave her husband, with whom she had known only
unhappiness, and live with her young lover. Was it bad of her to
have such thoughts? I told her this was not for me to decide and
asked her why she felt she needed someone else's confirmation.

MRS. A I would like to leave, and my husband wouldn't even care.
    But such a decision is out of the question. I can't leave.
JM Can you tell me more about that?
MRS. A I'm so afraid of what my daughter would think!
JM What does this decision have to do with your daughter?
MRS. A Daughters never want their mothers to get divorced. Do
    they?
JM Perhaps the question is not there. Your daughter is a grown
    woman. Do you feel that decisions about your personal life
    should remain in your daughter's hands?
MRS. A Well . . . yes . . . I've never thought of it that way. How
    would most mothers feel?
JM Perhaps we have to make a distinction between yourself as a
    mother and yourself as a woman?
MRS. A (note of astonishment in tone of voice) Oh! I see what you
    mean. It doesn't really have anything to do with my daughter,
    does it?
(Silence.)
MRS. A There's just one other thing . . . I feel now that it's a stupid
    thought but I have to tell you. My doctor did say that ulcerative
    colitis was psychosomatic. I was afraid that my relationship
    with this man might cause me to have another attack.
JM As though it were a punishment?

MRS. A Exactly! As a matter of fact, I think that was the main reason I came to see you. But I'm beginning to see things differently. I believed I was being disloyal to my daughter, taking something away from her.

JM As though you could not love this man and also still love your daughter?

MRS. A Yes. I suppose that's an utterly ridiculous idea.

JM Ideas that we feel strongly about are never "utterly ridiculous." Even if they are erroneous they have some meaning.

Now that she had been able to put into words her fantasy that ulcerative colitis was a form of punishment for sexual wishes I was able to show her that she believed somewhere inside herself that she had no right to pleasure in a love relationship. She agreed and then said that this new relationship was one of the greatest discoveries of her life. She had never understood during her childhood and adolescence that this was something to look forward to; she had thought that if love and sexual pleasure existed, they were not for her.

Mrs. A was then able to tell me something about her close tie with her *own* mother. She painted a highly idealized portrait in which details pointing to extremely negative feelings seemed totally split off from her consciousness. It became clear to me that she had invested her daughter with many of her mother's characteristics, as well as assigning to her a maternal role. The fact that her daughter had been conceived as soon as she left home may have served to mask what I presume to have been a profound inability to separate from her mother, perhaps even to recognize that she and her mother were not one fused person. When her mental image of the couple she formed with her daughter was suddenly severed, it seemed as though a hole had been rent in her unconscious image of herself. Unable to tolerate or even allow herself to recognize the feelings this aroused, she threw herself in desperation into increased professional activity, at the same time setting in motion the terrifying hemorrhaging that nearly took her life. But her mind knew nothing of this; only her body cried out in despair.

We discussed a little further what she had communicated regarding her relationship to her mother, as well as to her daughter as a

mother substitute, and her tendency, of which she had been unaware, to make them responsible for her adult life and well-being
as though she were still a little child. She responded, "You have
helped me see things clearly for the first time. I think that I can
assume my own choices about my life as a woman. After all, I'm
no longer a child!"

She went on to say that she was now convinced that she did not
need psychotherapy. I felt she would be capable of continuing on
her own to think about the *neurotic* aspects of her relationships.
However,there remained the much graver anxieties that lay behind
her threatening psychosomatic malady; these she unquestionably
did not wish to explore further. Behind these manifestations were
almost certainly many primitive anxieties linked to emotions of
rage and terror of abandonment, of which she had no knowledge.
In addition, these were in a sense the reasons her surgeon wished
her to consult a psychoanalyst. He was not aware of her neurotic
problem concerning her right to make her own decisions about her
love life, which, she now admitted, was the only reason she had
agreed to come and see me.

Since Mrs. A was adamant about not needing psychotherapy
and was doubtful about wanting a second interview, I felt I should
respect her decision. After all, perhaps she knew best. From what I
had been able to observe of her ways of functioning psychically, I
surmised that she had constructed deep defenses against archaic
anxieties concerning fantasies of bodily and mental fragmentation
as against becoming aware of other primitive emotional states. To
shake these structures without her express wish could be dangerous. At the same time I feared that, if there were any rift between
herself and her lover, this might unconsciously arouse the primitive
anxieties originally attached to separation from her mother, similar to the way in which they had undoubtedly been reactivated
toward her daughter.

I told her simply to remember that important relationships
probably stirred up much greater and more violent feelings than
she was aware of, and suggested that, in the event of any tension or
difficulties arising between herself and her man friend, she should

try to think about what she was feeling and not simply plunge into endless activity as a way of dealing with mental pain. She must not let her body "do all the feeling and thinking." She replied, "If that should happen, and after all couples do break up, I shall get in touch with you." A year later she wrote to tell me that she was in excellent health and that her personal and professional affairs were progressing satisfactorily.

For some 20 years Mrs. A had managed to remain totally unaware of the intense demand she made upon her daughter to complete her own sense of self and to make her feel that her life was worth living. She was equally unaware of her rage and despair when her grown daughter, in pursuit of her adult life—studies and marriage—left her mother to her own unhappy marriage. We might say that Mrs. A had created a "psychosomatic" mourning process for her immense loss. Mentally bleeding, she had nevertheless found another who was perhaps capable of healing the wound, but she had to come close to death before this solution could be found. The fact that she had been able to discover her "need to be loved" and also to question her apparently ungratifying marriage was an encouraging indication of her being in touch with her psychic reality. But she had little curiosity about her inner self, no doubt because of her resistance to what she suspected might be uncovered.

Let us now listen to the account of another "psychosomatic couple," which may convey further aspects of mother-child dependencies in relationship to psychosomatic phenomena. The profound influence that the fantasy of fusional identity may wield over both partners is also tragically displayed here.

On the advice of a colleague of mine, Mrs. B had phoned to say she needed urgently to talk to someone about her son. She insisted that the problem was so complicated she could tell me nothing more by telephone.

MRS. B I've worried about Bobby all my life. He was very intelligent but always so nervous. I couldn't let him go to holiday camps like the other children. Now, of course, he just does whatever he wants.

To my surprise I learn that Bobby is 28 years old! When Mrs. B left the United States because her husband's work brought him to Paris, Bobby was already 10. He never felt happy in France and constantly talked of returning to the States when he was older.

MRS. B I worked with him all the time on his school work and "we" got really good results. But he always slept badly and was reluctant to spend time with other children. He was very overweight. They called him "Fatty."

When I asked Mrs. B why she — not Bobby — had come to see me, she began, spontaneously, to tell me something about herself.

MRS. B I'm not in good health and I have to be careful. I've suffered most of my life from chronic ulcerative colitis. Worry makes it worse. It comes and goes, but usually I can get it under control with medication. When Bobby was 21 he was appointed to a very promising job in the States. Shortly after he left I had the most severe outbreak of ulcerative colitis that I've ever known. The doctors thought I was going to die and got in touch with my son. He returned instantly of course, and miraculously the hemorrhaging stopped two days later! He never went back.

Mrs. B then told me the reason for her present visit. She had recently discovered through a friend that her son was taking heroin. His work in an artistic field "allowed him too much liberty" in his mother's eyes. He would become angry when she attempted to find out how he was doing and had recently flown into "an unaccountable rage" because she had asked the young woman with whom he lived for news of him. She added, as though it were one more symptom, that this couple had a year-old son. When I told Mrs. B that there was little to be done if her son, who was no longer a child, saw no reason to consult anyone, she looked extremely upset. This led me to ask if she wanted to talk of her own anxiety about him and the feeling that she had no control over his actions. However, Mrs. B showed no inclination to explore this question. It seemed she had told me everything she had intended to tell me. I proposed tentatively that our relationships with our children sometimes parallel our relationships with our own parents. She then confided that her own mother, who had died shortly before she (Mrs. B) married, was a wonderful woman who found the solution to every problem. (I wondered whether she had come to see me in the hope that I would be like her mother in this respect.) I gave her the address of a treatment center and the names of several specialists in case she managed to convince her son to seek help, as well as an address where she could meet other mothers with similar problems.

My colleague later informed me that Mrs. B did not follow the indications for helping her son to get treatment or for getting help herself. Although it was evident that Mrs. B was deeply concerned about her son, this news did not surprise me. Bobby was, in a sense, her "symptom," but she was unable to see her relation to Bobby in this light or to take steps that might genuinely help Bobby towards treatment. Instead she put pressure on Bobby to come back to live with her. Two years later I learned that Bobby had committed suicide, but that Mrs. B was keeping well. Bobby's companion had turned to her for financial aid (which she was in a position to give), but she proposed that the young mother find work, and instead Mrs. B took over the total care of Bobby's son.

Although I never met Bobby and had only the briefest acquaintance with his mother, the news of his suicide left me feeling extremely sad and brought vividly to mind my difficult interview with Mrs. B. The sequence of events had the appearance of an inescapable destiny, as though, between Bobby and his mother, there could be only one life for the two of them.

Both Mrs. A and Mrs. B felt "torn" when their only child became an adult and left the family (in both cases for a far-off country). The kind of relationship that they maintained with their children was familiar to me through my work with other severely somatizing patients. In earlier writing I had referred to this kind of relationship as that of "the chasmic mother and the cork-child" (McDougall, 1982a, Chapter 4). The case illustration used in that chapter followed the psychoanalytic adventure of the "cork-child," since it was he, not the mother, who suffered from psychosomatic impairment. In such fusional relationships it is probable that neither mother nor child has been able to take full psychic possession of the body or of the individual self and that both are potentially threatened with either psychological or psychosomatic symptoms.

Since I did not have the opportunity to meet the grown children of Mrs. A or Mrs. B, I cannot know what *their* feelings about this close mother tie may have been, nor can I determine the extent to which this tie may have led Mrs. A's daughter to take flight into marriage and to live far from her family, and may have contributed to the death of Mrs. B's son. However, in the next chapter we shall have the occasion to follow the psychoanalytic voyage of an adult patient whose mother (as seen through her daughter's eyes) displayed in many ways the same intense maternal investment that Mrs. A and Mrs. B described toward their children. It is perhaps an important factor that, in all three cases, the mother affirmed that she had never wished for more than one child, as though this child were destined to fulfill a unique function for the mother, perhaps helping to patch up severe gaps in the mother's sense of individual identity — a problem that leads us to take into consideration the interrelating factors concerning three generations.

CHAPTER 5

Of Sleep and Death

As ALREADY MENTIONED, it is normal for a mother to regard her newborn baby as a narcissistic extension of herself and to feel merged with her infant. This permits her to interpret in her own way her baby's states of distress and consequently decide what it is feeling or needing. In the same way mothers intuitively seek to protect their babies from the impingement of overwhelming environmental stimuli. But some mothers (like Mrs. A and Mrs. B quoted in the last chapter) continue, for unconscious reasons, to experience their children, long past infancy, as a part of themselves. When there is little potential psychic "space" between mother and child (as may arise when the mother feels an anxious need to control her offspring's thoughts, emotions, and fantasies), then the growing child, lacking this vital space, may have difficulty organizing its own psychic reality and performing caretaking functions for itself.

These breakdowns in the communication between baby and mother frequently become apparent in the first months of life.

Nurslings invariably express psychological conflict in psychosomatic ways, the earliest signs being an alteration in one of the
fundamental physiological functions, such as breathing, digesting,
evacuating, and sleeping. Baby psychosomatic disorders may arise
in any of these vital functions, but I shall refer here only to infantile sleep disturbances. There are several reasons for this choice:
Infantile insomnia is a common phenomenon; the sleep-wake cycle
is a sensitive guide to early ego development; in the capacity to fall
asleep and keep asleep we may discern the earliest prototype of
psychic activity; and finally, this capacity is a privileged illustration of the psychic functioning of infants, and is considered by
research workers in this field to be a model for all early psychosomatic pathology (Fain, Kreisler, and Soulé, 1974).

Life-threatening infantile insomnia usually manifests itself in
the first weeks of life, the babies in question sleeping only three to
four hours in a 24 hour cycle. Many of these infants also display
motor discharge of a self-destructive kind in which they damage
themselves physically. The capacity to sleep, as well as the eventual
ability to dream, cannot be reduced to a purely neurobiological
level of functioning. (In the cases studied by the above-mentioned
authors, of which one is a noted pediatrician, careful preliminary
examination takes into account first, organic disturbance; second,
life conditions such as noise or unsuitable nourishment that may
interfere with normal infant sleep; third, psycho-affective disturbances.) Even though, in the first weeks of life, sleeping and waking
are closely tied to biological needs (that is, hunger awakens the
infant and satisfaction puts it to sleep), the act of falling asleep,
and particularly that of maintaining sleep, must be *libidinally invested* if the baby is to attain not only physical but also mental
health. Both falling asleep and sleeping itself must be experienced
as activities that bring the baby an inner sense of well-being. If
instead the infant experiences falling asleep as a state of anguished
abandonment, then it will be at risk for sleep disturbancs.

Fain (1971; Fain et al., 1974) delineates two forms of baby sleep
patterns: In the first of these patterns the baby is led, through a
feeling of contentment and fusion with its mother, into a libidinal
state of inner peacefulness which, following Freud (1900), we

might call primary narcissism. The second sleep pattern is preceded by an experience of frustration, distress, and painful tension, with the infant falling asleep from sheer exhaustion. The latter is purely physiological sleep, while the former is profoundly permeated with libidinal and narcissistic elements.

Freud's research into the psychology of dreams (1900) led him to postulate that when we fall asleep one part of the libido refuses to regress to the dreamless state of primary narcissism. This part sets in motion the hallucinatory process that is the essence of dreaming. Its function, according to Freud's theory, is to deal with the frustrated needs and exciting or frightening wishes that would otherwise disturb the sleeping individual. In view of the fact that the neurobiological conditions for hallucinatory activity exist from birth (and even before, since the REM cycles can be detected in the fetus), it must be supposed that severe infantile insomnia is a sign that the baby is unable to put into action the normal libidinal and narcissistic retreat from the world for which it is biologically programmed. If organic problems and disturbing environmental conditions are ruled out by the pediatrician, he is likely to assume that he is dealing with a pathological parent-infant relationship.

In this context we might well ask why certain infants appear unable to internalize the mother's role as the guardian of sleep. Instead these restless babies continually seek from the external world the source of libidinal and narcissistic contentment that should reign in their internal psychic world. The psychic energy expressed in libidinal and object-seeking activity has a disorganizing effect on both psychological and somatic levels of development, with potentially lethal consequences. The circuit of restless crying, tossing and head-banging is only stopped when the mother once again takes her baby into her arms and rocks it. The research of Fain, Kreisler and Soulé (1974) reveals that such mothers display two distinct modes of relationship to their infants: On the one hand, we find mothers who appear to invest their babies with overwhelming narcissistic interest leading to constant overstimulation; on the other we find mothers who express markedly inadequate interest in the baby giving rise to excessive frustration. A certain number of the mothers observed displayed a swing between these two positions, plunging the infant into an evident state of incoherence.

From the research on sleep disturbances in early infancy we might postulate that, once organic and environmental factors have been ruled out, it is the quality of the mother's narcissistic investment in her baby that determines the quality of her infant's sleep. When the internalization of the quasi-fusional mother-infant universe breaks down, the baby's physiological needs fail to become libidinally linked internally, and consequently will not function normally.

To sum up, the baby who can sleep only while being rocked in its mother's arms has been unable to build up an internal image of the mother which would allow it to sleep normally and peacefully after feeding. Normal sleep requires a mother who not only has an internal world that permits her to fuse narcissistically with her baby during the nursing period, but also wants her baby to do without her for a certain number of hours; this implies a mother who gives normal importance to other aspects of her adult life — her love life, her professional or homemaking interests, and her social life.

If the baby is destined to become the mother's sole object of libidinal and narcissistic satisfactions, there is a high risk of early perturbation; we may also predict a breakdown at a later stage in the maturation of the transitional phenomena designated by Winnicott (1951). This, in turn, will predispose the adult-to-be to the creation of what I have termed pathological transitional objects or "transitory objects" (McDougall 1982a). These may take the form of addictive substances, addictive relationships, and perverse or addictive sexual behavior. Addictive patterns seek to disperse mental pain and psychic conflict, as the mother did in infancy. They are also magical attempts to fill the void in the inner world, where a representation of a self-soothing maternal figure is lacking, and restore, if only briefly, the primitive dyadic ideal, in which all affective arousal ceases.

An addictive psychic economy is sometimes allied with psychosomatic dysfunctioning, since both tendencies have similar origins. The following psychoanalytic vignette, taken from the analysis of a patient whose symptoms included lifelong insomnia as well as eczema and incipient alcoholism in adulthood, may serve to illustrate some of the far-reaching consequences of this early lack of an internalized maternal caretaking introjected object.

The following are my notes from the first preliminary interviews:

Sophie, a 26-year-old psychiatrist, holds an important post for her age. She makes an urgent plea for help because of depression and increasing alcoholism. Her drinking problems began in early adolescence; from the age of 11 she stole whiskey from her parents and would drink a glass when she felt tense or restless. She is devoted to the patients she treats in a hospital setting but is afraid that her tension and need to drink may eventually affect her work. She has already had two serious car accidents due to drunken driving.

She is also seeking to understand the failures in her love relationships. Exclusively homosexual, she has no wish to become heterosexual, but dreams of being able to create more stable relationships. Every love affair breaks down. She makes excessive demands on lovers' time, is always striving to "make them over," to "repair all that they have lacked in childhood," but also, at times, "seeks to humiliate them" for reasons she does not understand. With regard to her sexual life she added that only the pleasure of her partners counts for her. She herself cannot stand to be caressed in any way. The presence of a lover at night is very important, since *she is quite unable to fall asleep if alone.*

This led us to talk about her insomnia. Throughout her life she remembered having difficulty in falling asleep and once asleep would tend to wake up frequently with feelings of terror but no memory of any dreams. Her parents often refer to her serious insomnia as a small baby. "According to my mother, she could never put me down. I would immediately begin to bawl. She said I practically never slept except when she rocked me in her arms." Both parents retain the impression that for six months after her birth they themselves hardly slept because Sophie would scream, claw at herself, and rock in her crib. After this period the insomnia receded and Sophie began to sleep more normally but always very lightly. She also suffered from infant asthma and certain food allergies, but these had disappeared by the time she was ten.

These reminiscences led Sophie to talk of her parents. She is the only child of an Italian working-class father and a French mother of bourgeois extraction. Both had a rigid Catholic upbringing. Her father was particularly stern regarding sexual matters. (I learned later that he would recount with pride how he had once publicly struck his 17-year-old sister because she was holding hands with a young man.) "I understood pretty early that, as far as my father is concerned, all women are evil." Over the years her father has built up a highly lucrative enterprise. "He's very generous — keeps offering me money — but I get the feeling he's trying to buy my affection. . . . He pays little attention to my mother, as though she were my responsibility. Always goes off saying, 'Take care of your mother. You're the man of the family now.' I got so tired of trying to meet all her demands for my presence. In the end he gave me the money to buy my present apartment — but I'm going to reimburse all of it!"

Sophie's mother has always insisted that the father's family was far inferior to her own. Her mother, too, constantly made denigrating remarks about sexual and love relations, as well as about "woman's lot." "They seemed to expect me to lead a sexless life. When I told them I was homosexual my father acted disdainfully, but my mother accepted it very calmly." Sophie describes her mother as having always been excessive in her concern about Sophie's eating, cleanliness, and toilet training. Throughout her childhood and adolescence she received frequent enemas and many kinds of medication for unknown reasons. Her mother often talked of the difficulty that raising children presented. Before Sophie's birth she had been pregnant with twin boys who were stillborn at term. "She swore after I was born that she would never have another child." (Later it became clear that Sophie believed she had been born with the wrong sex, and in addition had the fantasy that she should be the equal of two boys.)

At the end of our second meeting, when I asked Sophie if there was anything else she wanted to tell me, she said that she had suffered for the last ten years from eczema but that she did not feel it was important enough to mention. Her reluctant statement discouraged further questioning on my part, although I must admit that I was curious to know more, since I had had another patient, also homosexual, who had her first outbreak of eczema during a homosexual love affair. This had led to several suppositions on my part, which I have recounted elsewhere (McDougall 1982a, Chapter 1).

From these initial interviews I surmised that Sophie's parents both suffered from considerable inner distress and neurotic anxiety, and that her mother was possibly struggling also with psychotic anxieties attached to bodily functions, which she projected onto her daughter. Whether these suppositions were true or not, this was the way Sophie experienced the internal images of her parents. Consequently, in spite of her irritation with her parents due to their invasiveness and continual demands upon her, she spent much of her life trying to "repair" them in her own way. Not only was she an assiduous "family doctor" to them and to their various relatives, but in unconscious ways, as I came to learn later, her professional choices and her sexual preference were also a response to what she felt they demanded of her.

Her intelligence and her profound suffering led me to accept her for analysis, although I felt dubious about the therapeutic results that might be attained considering the archaic terror I sensed behind her manifest symptomatology.

Analysis began some months later on a four times weekly basis and continued for six years. Towards the end of the first year Sophie allowed herself to speak of her first outbreak of eczema. During adolescence she had had her first sexual experience during her adolescence with an admired woman teacher in her school. The following day her right hand and her arm were covered with a massive eruption that was red and irritating. Later in the week the family doctor diagnosed eczema. Ever since this time, there have been recurrent outbreaks on her right hand, but these could not be linked to a distinct experience as on the first occasion. Sophie, of course, interpreted her dermatological eruption as a somatic punishment for sexual guilt. While this was no doubt a plausible interpretation, we also discovered as the analysis progressed that exac-

erbation of Sophie's eczema coincided not only with the enacting
of forbidden incestuous wishes (in which her lovers played the role
of the longed-for mother of infancy who held her eternally in her
arms) but also, and perhaps above all, with unsuspected rage and
destructive anger towards her lovers. Behind these manifestations
in the present we came to discern that Sophie sought in her partners the idealized image of her mother, while the equally strong
hatred had been split off and totally disavowed.

When Sophie felt I was unable to bring her inner peace and
confidence in her desperately needed right to live and to love, the
anger would became attached to the analytic relationship. We
traced the origins of these transference manifestations to many
searing memories of Sophie's relationship with her mother. Having
always maintained an idealized image of her devoted mother, she
now added a second representation based on her conviction that
her mother "wanted total physical and mental control" over her.
On one occasion, while talking of her intense interest in learning
other languages, she said, "My mother is only interested in dead
languages, . . . I think this is the language she reserved for me.
. . . I was not intended to take my place among the living, but to
live inside her head."

Around this time Sophie recounted an important element from
her past that had bearing on her insomnia and in particular on the
need to have a female partner near her in order to sleep. "I was
nine years old when my parents allowed me to have a separate
room. It was just opposite theirs and mother never allowed me to
close my bedroom door. She fixed a mirror to her own door which
was also kept open, so that she could watch me at any time to see
what I was doing or if I were sleeping. She kept this mirror-watch
on me until I was well into my teens. From the time of my first
homosexual relationship I slammed my door shut every night when
I went to bed." She concluded, "I know she loved me, yet at the
same time her hands of iron were squeezing the life out of me."
Sophie's love and hate for her mother were epitomized in these
memories. She both demanded this constant attention and feared
it as a lethal enthrallment. It became evident that the hands of love

and iron wished not only to caress and possess but also to strangle and lacerate.

Such feelings are not sufficient explanation for Sophie's eczema, which cannot be equated with an hysterical symptom. Nevertheless, the fact that the eczema occurred only on her hands suggests symbolism of a primitive pregenital kind. Perhaps once more one might think in terms of an archaic form of hysteria, in which verbal links and a consolidated body image play a minor role. It seems probable that if Sophie had had access to her aggressive and violent fantasies at the level of verbal thought, she would not have suffered from this symptom.

While talking of feelings of abandonment and desolation evoked in relationships with a lover, Sophie would make movements as though to claw at her hands. This made me wonder if she were reliving in her body the feelings of the distressed infant who clawed at herself in her crib, desperately searching for the missing mother. However this may be, her eczema slowly cleared up as this underlying dimension of anger and terror attached to her relation to her mother could be put into words, and did not recur during the remaining years of her analysis.

Sophie's alcoholism was also an attempt to take flight from intolerable affective states of anger and abandonment that she could neither contain nor elaborate. She had little tolerance for the mental pain caused by strong negative feelings; in fact, during the first three years of our work together, she would constantly turn to alcohol as a means of reducing tensions of this kind. She refused the advice of her colleagues to join Alcoholics Anonymous, saying that she was determined to gain analytic understanding into the reasons for her fragility. Little by little we achieved this aim, with the result that her drinking no longer presented a suicidal threat. It was noteworthy that, during these three years, no matter how distressed, tense or ill she felt, Sophie never once abandoned her patients, and constantly put their needs before her own. Although this dedication was invaluable in her professional activity, Sophie's neglect of the distressed and needy child within herself constituted something of a narcissistic hemorrhage.

By dint of hard analytic work on her violently ambivalent feelings toward her sexual partners, she was at last able to create a
stable love relationship with a somewhat younger woman who
appeared to need Sophie's strength, advice, and caring. Nevertheless, she herself felt overdependent on her lover and suffered from
severe anxiety attacks and insomnia whenever Beatrice was obliged
to be absent in the course of her work. Sophie's desperate need was
apparent when she confided that if the pain became too great she
would take her life. She had a small box of pills ready for this
contingency. I asked her to give them into my keeping; she was very
moved by this request but refused. At one point an incident of
infidelity on Beatrice's part led her to contrive elaborate plans to
kill her lover and even to buy the revolver with which to carry out
her violent plan. This was a tense and terrible time for both Sophie
and myself. I treated her project as a paranoid delusion, and
Sophie slowly came round to seeing it this way also. As a result she
was able to win back Beatrice's love and her life slowly settled into
place once more. For circumstantial reasons which again awakened
the fear of losing her lover, whom she felt to be life itself, she
finally decided to move with Beatrice away from Paris.

One year later I received a letter from Sophie telling me her
friend had abandoned her. She recalled her old murderous project
but said that she would now be incapable of putting it into action.
I wrote asking her to come back to see me and she replied that she
would not "allow me to breathe hope into her once more." Two
months later she took her own life.

I learned that before taking this desperate step, apparently,
Sophie had left a letter for her parents (as she had once intimated
to me she would do), assuring them of her devotion but explaining
that she could not live without Beatrice. The parents nevertheless
refused to believe that the loss of her lover was the precipitating
cause of Sophie's suicide. They were unable to understand that
Beatrice had become invested as a vital mother substitute and that
her departure left Sophie feeling as empty and distraught as she
had been in infancy, tossing and screaming in her crib, unable to
sleep, and now, without either an internal or an external mother to
soothe her, wishing only for death.

Wanting to contact people who had been important to Sophie, her parents sent the reproduction of a photo of their daughter announcing their sad loss. I received a copy. They had chosen a somewhat tragic portrait but one which reflected well Sophie's air of intensity and gravity. However, to my shock I discovered that, where one would have expected birthdate and day of death, the parents, perhaps distracted by their grief, had given dates that appeared to indicate that Sophie lived only from the day of her death to the day of her burial, some five days later! I reflected sadly that it was as though their daughter, so intensely invested narcissistically by both of them, had never truly been granted separate existence. It was perhaps too much to expect that they would understand that Sophie's homosexuality was her only protection against self-destruction. She was loved and hated as a part of themselves, rather than as a separate individual with her own needs and desires, and perhaps only achieved independent status in their eyes at the moment she took her life — an act which they had not planned and over which they had no control.

Perhaps this tragic error on the part of Sophie's parents, concerning her birthdate and the date of her death, may convey something of the unsuspected deathlike forces that are apt to pass from one generation to another, and may communicate, even to young infants, the conviction that their destiny is to accept non-existence as separate beings in their parents' eyes. The defenses marshalled to deal with this threat of psychic annihilation leads many adults — through drug abuse, alcoholism, suicide and psychosomatic deaths — to fulfill what they had unconsciously believed as children was their only road to freedom.

CHAPTER 6

Affects, Affect Dispersal, and Disaffectation

I T IS PERHAPS ADVISABLE at this point to bring together what has already transpired regarding affective experience and its relationship to psychosomatic disorders, as well as its role in the problems of addiction. The preceding chapters have demonstrated, through the use of clinical illustrations, the extent to which certain people manage, in particular circumstances, to pulverize all trace of strong feeling, so that an experience which has caused emotional flooding is not recognized as such and therefore cannot be contemplated. (This was the case with Mrs. A, described in Chapter 4, when her daughter left home.)

The psychic economy of affect, as well as the unconscious reasons that lead certain individuals to render much of their emotional experience lifeless, first became a subject of interest and observation for me because of my countertransference reactions to those of my analysands who suffered from this kind of destruction of affective experience. In many cases their psychoanalytic process seemed to stagnate for long periods of time—or even appeared never to have begun. The analysands themselves frequently complained that "nothing was happening" in their analytic adventure, yet each clung to his analysis like a drowning man to a life preserver. The mute appeal that I managed to discern through the accusations and denigrations directed toward me made me want to discover *who*, in my analysand's inner psychic world, was begging to be understood in his or her expression of hopelessness. Although the patients of whom I am thinking had sought analytic help for a variety of reasons, they had one personality feature in common: Their relationships with others were often presented in an unemotional or utilitarian way, almost as though they had to deny the importance of depending on another person. It is evident that the psychoanalytic relationship will present problems of a painful narcissistic nature to patients who have difficulty in admitting a need for help. (The vignette from the analysis of Jack Horner, quoted in Chapter 7, provides an obvious example of this kind of mental pain.)

As time went on, some of these patients made me feel paralyzed in my analytical functioning. I could neither help them to become more alive nor lead them to terminate analysis. The affectless quality of certain sessions made me feel weary, and I would find my attention wandering. In addition, their spectacular lack of analytic progress made me feel guilty.

AN EXAMPLE OF DIAGNOSTIC FAILURE

I am reminded here of a patient from northern Europe whose husband's work had brought her to France. She claimed she felt angry most of the time. She asserted two reasons for this: "In any aspect of life no woman could be happy in a man's world," and "no citizen of whatever country could be happy living among the French, with the way they carry on." I told her that at the end of the analysis (for she insisted this was what she needed) she would still be a woman and the French would carry on the way they always do. We had three interviews before she came to accept that there was—perhaps—something in her way of experiencing her femininity and—perhaps—a clash of cultural and social differ-

ences that could be endured with less pain. Only then did I feel
that she was potentially analyzable.

In any case it was a disastrous error of judgment on my part,
since throughout her work with me Kate was convinced that I was
sick. My sickness of mind lay in the fact that I failed to realize or
to acknowledge how tragic it was to be born a woman and how
impossible the French really were. But she was determined to have
an analysis because someone she admired had had one and had
become rich, presumably as a result of therapy. Although she did
not become rich, Kate did discover a new hobby of an artistic
nature, which brought her considerable pleasure. Yet she continued to feel that life had dealt her a rotten deal and that she might
well have made her discovery without the aid of analysis. I had
accepted Kate for treatment partly because I was a very young
analyst, eager to work, and convinced that anyone who asked for
analysis deserved it. She manifested severe obsessional symptoms,
which I had been taught were "a good indication" for psychoanalytic treatment (but which, as it turned out, did not interest her as
an object of analytic investigation). Then again, she had cried
when I first mentioned her "painful feelings about being a woman," and I interpreted this as an appeal for help in experiencing her
femininity differently. As time went on, I tried also to interest her
in discovering the underlying causes of her sexual frigidity. "Ridiculous! Everyone knows that only men enjoy sex!" she once retorted
when I asked if her lack of sexual pleasure were a problem for her.
We came to understand that her exasperation with her husband,
her children and myself was of the same nature as her exasperation
with the French but this discovery led nowhere. I did not suspect at
this time that change itself was terrifying to patients like Kate. No
doubt I was also blinded by my own wish that Kate should enjoy
being a woman and was unable to reach the profound gulf of
despair to which she clung with violence and anger.

Unable to analyze to my own satisfaction these countertransference affects in face of Kate's continually negative therapeutic
reaction to our work, and in spite of the many notes I took on our
work together, I began to feel as disappointed with her as she with
me. Inspired by my failure, I managed to survive the experience by

writing about what I had understood of my difficult analytic encounter with Kate. In my first attempt to conceptualize this way of
mental functioning, I referred, rather ungraciously, to patients
who resembled Kate as "anti-analysands in analysis" (McDougall,
1972) because they seemed to be in fierce opposition to analyzing
anything to do with their inner psychic world, insisting on external
reality as the only dimension of interest. I would say today that this
paper inadequately explores the depth of despair and the experience of inner death that lie behind the suffering and angry protestation of patients like Kate, rendering them resistant to psychic
change, since they believe profoundly that change can only be for
the worse. Immobility is felt to be the only protection against a
return to an unbearable and inexpressible traumatic state. Whether
Kate would have agreed to explore such feelings and whether this
would have rendered her less impervious to the psychoanalytic
process I am unable to know.

A certain number of such patients (although not all) were considered by others and considered themselves to be eminently "normal." This led me later to refer to them as "normopaths," that is,
as individuals who, while deeply disturbed, seemed to seek shelter
behind a wall of "pseudo-normality" that was relatively devoid of
awareness of emotional experience (McDougall 1982a). However, I
was unable to see further into this curious condition, except to
conjecture that it was probably rather widespread among the population at large, and might well characterize what many would
refer to as "normal people."

Later, I discovered that, behind the apparently angry protesta-
tions of these analysands, they were in fact suffering from a striking *absence of affect*. The word that seemed most appropriate to
describe them was that they were "disaffected." In coining this
term I hoped to indicate that such people had in fact experienced
overwhelming emotion that threatened to attack their sense of
integrity and identity. This hypothesis challenged the theory of
neuroanatomical defects, based on observations made in psychosomatic centers, as an explanatory hypothesis to account for the
phenomenon of alexthymia. I came to the conclusion that my
patients, unable to repress the ideas linked to emotional pain and

equally unable to project these feelings delusionally onto the representations of other people, simply ejected them from consciousness. They were not suffering from an inability to experience or express emotion, but from an inability to contain and reflect over an *excess* of affective experience. When the phenomenon of disaffectation occurs, the individual runs the risk of an impaired capacity for dreaming (as in the case of Christopher discussed in Chapter 3 and of many other patients who suffer from insomnia) and of psychosomatic breakdown.

At present I have some hypotheses to propose regarding the mental functioning that contributes to this disaffected state. These deal, first, with the dynamic reasons that may underlie the maintenance of a psychic gap between emotions and the mental representations to which they are attached, and second, with the economic means by which this affectless way of experiencing events and people functions. It is difficult to avoid the conclusions that such an ironclad structure must be serving some highly important defensive function, and that its continuous maintenance will involve vigorous psychic activity, even if the patients concerned have no conscious knowledge of this and the analyst little observable material upon which to found such an opinion.

AFFECT DISPERSAL OR THE ADDICTIVE SOLUTION

In some cases affective reactions are not evident in the analytic sessions because the patients in question are constantly engaged in immediately *dispersing in action* the impact of certain emotional experiences. As often as not this applies to pleasurable as well as painful affects. Let us now examine in more detail the discharge-in-action mechanism that rules the psychic economy, when this phenomenon occurs.

Many years ago a patient, the mother of a little psychotic boy called Sammy (who provided me with the vivid experience that was published in *Dialogue with Sammy*, McDougall and Lebovici, 1960), turned to me for help shortly after her son's return to the United States. She missed Sammy very much and feared her alcoholism would increase. She felt so "empty" without him. When trying to describe her feelings about this unhappy situation she would say, "I can never tell whether I'm hungry or angry or anxious or wanting sex—and that's when I start to drink." Although a very young and inexperienced analyst, I realized that she seemed incapable of reflecting on emotional events. I began to wonder whether addictive behavior might aim at clouding from consciousness experiences an individual felt unable to bear because the strength of the feelings and their conflictual nature aroused confusion. Many years later, when I came across the concept of alexithymia, I immediately recognized the phenomenon that I had observed—the inability to distinguish one affect from another. Some patients were alexithymic in the sense that they appeared to be unaware of important emotional upsurges; others, like Sammy's mother, were conscious of strong feelings but would immediately *disperse* these through engaging in action of some kind or another. In this way they evacuated the unbearable affective arousal.

We are all liable to discharge tension in "acting-out" ways when events are unusually stressful (eating, drinking, smoking more than usual, etc.). But those who *habitually* use action as a defense against mental pain (when thought and the recognition of feeling would be more appropriate) run the risk of increasing their psychosomatic vulnerability. An affect cannot be conceived as a purely mental or purely physical event. *Emotion is essentially psychosomatic.* Thus, ejecting the psychological part of an emotion allows the physiological part to express itself as in infancy, leading to a resomatization of affect. The signal from the psyche is reduced to an action message devoid of words. Individuals who handle emotion in this way are likely victims for psychosomatic explosions when events such as accidents, births, deaths, divorces, and abandonments occur. At such times addictive solutions may also break down, so that the use of drugs or drug-like relationships ceases to offer this form of escape from psychological pressures and affective flooding.

Also, it is important to note that, with certain patients, these defensive screens against the awareness of affect or its rapid discharge in action might often pass unnoticed for many long months! Anxiety is the mother of invention in the psychic theater. Without its warning signals (because the painful representations are either immediately ejected or discharged in action), certain individuals run the risk of not knowing that they are feeling threatened psychologically. Thus the analyst may also be unaware that such analysands are not dealing with the problems that are facing them; that instead they become aware only of the overpowering need for medication, food, tobacco, alcohol, opiates, and so on. For others, frantic sexual exploits of a perverse or compulsive nature, in which the partner plays little role as a person but is used rather like a calming drug, may serve the same purpose. (These relationships will be discussed in more detail later in this chapter.)

Those who use *other people* (not necessarily sexual partners) as objects of addictive demands also present a similar psychic economy. Like a certain number of the analysands referred to above, these patients frequently complain of feeling empty, misunderstood or out of touch with others. In analysis they talk at great length of important people in their lives, usually complaining that they are rarely there when needed and are felt, therefore, to be unkind or neglectful to the dependent individual. These "others," who come into the category of the self-objects described by Kohut (1971), are used, like transitional objects, for the purposes of self-soothing or, just as often, as objects to be mastered and attacked. (This is also the fate of the true transitional object of childhood which is bitten, torn, and in various ways "punished" as much as it is " loved.") But, unlike the transitional object, addictively needed others fail to provide for more than a short time the comfort demanded, and what they offer is rarely enough for the desperate, raging infant hidden within these unhappy adults. They are unconsciously treated like the "breast mother" of infancy, who is held responsible for all the baby's pleasure, as well as all its pain. The "others" who allow themselves, unconsciously, to be manipulated into living out another individual's unacknowledged psychological crises have also found a characterological way of solving the same problem. This too often escapes notice in spite of the intensifying psychoanalytic microscope. (These forms of addictive relationship have been discussed in detail in McDougall, 1982a, Chapter 3.)

Others, like the cardiac patients described by William Osler (see Chapter 1), may indulge in what I have called an "activity addiction," that is, a drug-like relationship to their daily work or to numerous other activities (which sometimes do not even interest them), with the unconscious aim of leaving no room for relaxation or daydreaming. These people are continually involved in "doing" rather than in "being" or "experiencing." Such was part of the inner drama of Mrs. A discussed in Chapter 4.

Individuals who seek psychotherapeutic help for addictive problems are, of course, not typically alexithymic; even if their anxiety is quickly dispelled by the addictive solution (particularly in the case of substance abuse), they are still aware of the suffering that their dependence upon the addictive substance imposes on them.

The paradox presented by the addictive object is that, in spite of its sometimes death-dealing potential, it is always invested as a good object by some part of the mind. Whatever the object may be, it is inevitably endowed with the supreme quality of enabling the addicted person to rapidly dispel mental conflict and psychic pain, even if only briefly. In the same vein, we can understand why even affects of pleasure may mobilize the craving for the addictive object in these analysands, just as a small child in states of excitement needs its mother to act as a protective and filtering screen against emotional flooding. However, the soothing substance has to be sought ceaselessly in the external world, usually in increasing quantities. While it is, in fact, playing the role of the transitional objects of early childhood, it is not a true transitional object (or, if so considered, must be judged an extremely pathological one).

In indicating the similarity between addictive substances and transitional objects, I am drawing attention once again to the fact that people who function with an addictive psychic economy as a means of obliterating psychic pain lack an internal representation of the mother as a caretaking introject with whom to identify in states of tension or conflict. The internal fragility is further weakened, as already emphasized, by the equally important lack of a strong paternal introject.

In the course of analysis with such patients, we often discover that the mother was seen as being too emotionally fragile to play a coherent maternal role. She is frequently recalled as forbidding any display of emotion on the child's part, as though it were too much for her to bear. (Tim and Georgette, quoted in later chapters, both came to understand their mothers in this way; in consequence, much of their bitterness about the past was attenuated.) The subsequent lack of support from the father or his death (which to the bereaved child represents a cruel abandonment) can then also be understood and to a large extent accepted or pardoned.

The patient who seeks analysis in order to lose an addictive propensity poses a particular problem, for such an individual is frequently not seeking self-knowledge but power—a power stronger than his/her own which of course we are quite unable to promise. Psychoanalysis or psychoanalytic therapy replaces neither Alcoholics Anonymous nor a drug treatment center. Psychoanalytic treatment is potentially effective only if our addicted patient is eager to discover *why* he/she flies to the soothing substance at the slightest signal of stress. (Tim's struggle with a tobacco addiction that had become life-threatening, the details of which are recounted in Chapter 9, is a case in point.)

Let me emphasize that experiences of severing oneself from an addiction are rich in discovery in the course of the analytic voyage. Since relapses are the rule rather than the exception, the analysand may be interested in exploring the narcissistic and libidinal wounds that precipitate an addictive plunge. The analysis of such experiences may reveal the early traumatic experiences of infancy and the personality organization and psychic economy which subsequently developed, leaving the child (and the future adult) without adequate inner resources for coping with emotional flooding.

Sexuality as a Drug

Another aspect of the addictive solution, of quite a different order from substance abuse, is the above-mentioned pursuit of compulsive sexual discharge in times of stress. (For this type of relationship, in which the act rather than the partner is invested, I have coined the term "addictive sexuality" (McDougall 1982a,

1986). This concept evolved from analytic work with certain homosexual and heterosexual analysands. Many homosexuals have a
compulsive and addictive relationship to their partners, as do
many heterosexual patients, in the pursuit of what I have come to
call "neosexualities." These are complicated perverse scenarios,
frequently of a fetishistic or sadomasochistic nature, and sometimes performed alone, in which the sexual rituals are felt as a
drug-like necessity, destined to reassure their creator against anxiety concerning the loss of not only sexual but also subjective identity feeling.

To this category of sexual addicts should be added those hetero-
sexuals for whom sexuality has a compulsive and drug-like quality,
in that the partner plays little role in the subject's inner world,
being more an object of need than an object of desire. A remark
from the analysis of Jack Horner (whom we shall meet in the next
chapter) illustrates this kind of sexual experience. "I don't know
what you mean when you say I don't seem to truly *desire* a woman.
How can you desire someone who isn't there?" (This is a shining
example of operatory thinking and of a delibidinized way of relating to another.) The patient then went on to say that the important
thing about the sexual act was that it enabled him to sleep. Perhaps
for some people sex is mainly a sleeping pill. Such partnerships
may be relatively long-lasting, as long as the "sleeping-pill" does
not object to his/her role. The difficulty arises from the fact that
people like Jack are also terrified of close and continuing relationships and tend to destroy them in spite of their need-satisfying
aspects. In this they resemble certain homosexual men, who, although frequently clinging to the dream of finding someone they
can love and live with, are compelled constantly to change partners. The unconscious pressures against the realization of more
stable relationships lie not only in the fact that the sexual partner
frequently represents an object of consummation rather than another human being (the addictive dimension), but also in the fact
that they change partners as a protection against becoming aware
of unconscious castrating wishes toward the partner.

One might conclude that, in both homosexual and heterosexual
relationships, when the sexual partner is a "condition" rather than

a "person," there are profoundly menacing unconscious fantasies about love relationships. These include (but go beyond) classical castration fantasies. Fears of being possessed and damaged by the other are equaled only by unconscious fears of wishing to implode into and damage the partner or of losing one's individual identity by merging with the other.

On the psychoanalytic stage, as might be expected, analysands falling into any of these categories tend to become addicted to their psychoanalytic experience. The analyst runs the risk of becoming the object onto whom will be transferred the role of the disappointing mother universe that failed to be introjected, there to provide the possibility of self-soothing and self-care. It sometimes happens that patients with this problem are unable to make use of the analyst and his/her interpretations, but at the same time they are unable to give up the relationship in spite of their constantly renewed bitterness and disappointment. Some of these analysands have revealed that those in their entourage proclaim, to their chagrin, that they are much "improved," that is, much easier to live with. Meanwhile the analysand claims that the analyst is incompetent and uncaring and that the analysis is a failure.

Faced with such stalemate, analysts tend to feel paralyzed, as though their analytic functioning had been deadened. Thus, a feeling of inner death pervades the analytic relationship. We then become aware, through our countertransference experience, of death-seeking factors in our patients whose goal it is to freeze the current of life. This vitally important unconscious dimension has been masked hitherto by neurotic symptomatology and numerous addictive patterns of behavior.

METAPSYCHOLOGICAL CONSIDERATIONS

In attempting to better conceptualize the mental processes involved in the radical dispersal or compulsive discharge of affective experience, I was considerably helped by studying the research work of the analytically oriented psychosomaticists (Marty, de M'Uzan, and David, 1963; Marty and de M'Uzan, 1963; Nemiah and Sifneos, 1970). Curiously enough, those working in psychosomatic centers were the first to observe and construct hypotheses to explain the phenomenon of affectless ways of experiencing and communicating. Their research led to the delineation of a "psychosomatic personality," as well as to the economic and dynamic concepts of operatory thinking and alexithymia already described.

Although doubtful of the existence of a "psychosomatic personality" and of the validity of their concepts as far as my own patients were concerned (probably because we are dealing with two different populations and two different kinds of request for help), I was nevertheless helped through their work to become aware of the fact that the patients I had referred to as "normopaths," "addictive personalities," and "disaffected" people also frequently tended to somatize under stressful conditions. The psychosomatic reaction was usually due to a breakdown in their habitual ways of discharging affect or to an overwhelming of the alexithymic devices, whose defensive function (in my opinion) was the warding off of deep-seated anxieties of a psychotic type. The door was then open to psychosomatic dysfunctioning in response to a primitive signal from that part of the psyche that had no words to capture and contain the frightening fantasies in question.

Words are most effective containers for channeling the energy linked to instinctual drives, as well as the fantasies to which they have given birth, with regard to the parental objects of infancy. When words do not perform this function (for reasons that remain highly conjectural), the psyche is obliged to give distress signals of a presymbolic kind, thereby circumventing the restraining links of language. There is then a considerable risk of evoking somatic instead of psychological responses to the experience of wordless anguish.

The psychosomatic phenomena observable in a psychoanalytic setting inevitably give rise to concepts that differ from those arising from neurobiological fields of research, even when the patient population is similar, since these sciences are working on different theories of *causality* (McDougall, 1982a, Chapter 7). Psychoanalysis as a science is centered on meaning (and in particular on the meaning of relationships); its underlying logic is the logic of language. In attempting to conceptualize the body-mind relationship outside the role of language we must formulate at least one pivotal question: What defense mechanisms can the infantile psyche use to protect against the return of early traumatic experience and the reexperiencing of the accompanying anguish which might prove intolerable to the individual?

I have referred in earlier chapters to the importance, in my opinion, of the archaic mechanism (as detailed by Freud) of total "ejection" or "foreclosure from the psyche." Freud (1911b, 1915a, 1924, 1938a, 1938b) delineated three defense mechanisms that attempted to deny, undo or in other ways get rid of troubling experiences: Negation (*Verneinung*), denial or disavowal (*Verlengnung*), and foreclosure or repudiation from the psyche (*Verwerfung*). The last is the most elusive of the three concepts insofar as clinical applications are concerned. Freud considered the capacity of the psyche to completely *eject* an experience from consciousness (rather than keeping it in the form of repression) to be a typically psychotic manifestation. In the Schreber case (1911a) he demonstrates that what is repudiated from consciousness and not subsequently reintegrated into the subject's unconscious (in contrast to what occurs in repression) returns in the form of hallucinations or delusions. Therefore, the experiental traces that are left are not the same in foreclosure as they are in repression.

Based on my clinical experience, I would suggest that this capacity to foreclose certain perceptions, thoughts, fantasies, or other psychological events (frequently mobilized by current events in the external world) is operative in the adult's regression to psychosomatic rather than psychological responses to conflict and psychic pain. There is a dissociation between word-presentations and thing-presentations, so that the bodily signals of anxiety (that is, the *somatic* pole of affect) become equivalent to a thing-presentation, severed from the word-presentation that would give meaning to the experience. (It should be recalled that the infant experiences its body as an object belonging to the outside world.) Exploration of the historic reasons for this body-mind or thing-word split opens the way for many conjectural hypotheses concerning the earliest transactions between mother and infant. While we may never know what actually took place, we are able to witness the way in which the child's version of it is kept intact in the adult's way of thinking (or not thinking) and of functioning (or not functioning) in response to the everyday circumstances of life. This brings us back to a consideration of the term "disaffectation."

ON DISAFFECTATION

By "disaffectation" I hope to convey a double meaning. The Latin prefix *dis-*, which indicates "separation" or "loss," may suggest, metaphorically, that certain people are psychologically separated from their emotions and may indeed have "lost" the capacity to be in touch with their psychic realities. But I should also like to include in this neologism the significance of the Greek prefix *dys-* with its implications in regard to illness. However, I have avoided spelling the word in this way because I might then appear to have invented a malady. Although a brief could be held, with regard to affect pathology, for considering a total incapacity to be in touch with one's affective experience to be a grave psychological illness, in the long run such terms lead us to categorize people, with a consequent tendency to concretize our thinking, thus leaving it less open to further elaboration. The word "alexithymia," for example, has already been exposed to this inconvenience. Certain practitioners say, "This person is suffering from alexithymia," as though it were a definable illness rather than an observable but little understood phenomenon. I choose to speak of disaffectation rather than alexithymia for another reason. Although the two manifestations are, from a phenomenological viewpoint, similar, and the two fields of research from which they arise complementary, each field starts with different premises and is studying a different dimension of "psychosomatic" humankind.

ETIOLOGICAL CONSIDERATIONS

The extreme fragility, observable in the course of analysis, of the narcissistic economy of many addicted, disaffected, and somatizing analysands, linked to the incapacity to contain and to elaborate verbally numerous affective experiences, provides hypothetical answers regarding possible etiological factors. At the level of recall, there is frequently reference to a family discourse that promulgated an ideal of inaffectivity, as well as a condemnation of imaginative experience. Beyond these elements of conscious recall I have sometimes been able to reconstruct with my patients the existence of a paradoxical mother-child relationship in which the mother was felt to be out of touch with her child's emotional needs. Perhaps in response to her unconscious fear of her own affective life, she (in the analysand's memory) controlled to the utmost her child's thoughts, feelings, and spontaneous gestures. While we may never know just what transpired in the intimate bodily and psychological exchanges between mother and infant to render emotional experience unacceptable or lifeless, we are able to observe what happens when experiences charged with affect arise in the psychoanalytic relationship. Pulverized affect will sometimes come to light as part of the discovery of a lost continent in the inner psychic world.

To begin with, when there is a conspicuous lack of dreams and fantasies in circumstances that would normally produce such psychic activity, this is frequently replaced by somatic sensations and reactions. (The example of Christopher quoted in Chapter 3 is illustrative of this.) Secondly, when affect-laden ideas return to consciousness, the defenses against them may achieve expression in the form of transitory *pseudo-perceptions* rather than emotions that can be named and contemplated. These "dream equivalents," which often obey primary process thinking, may also be regarded as "affect equivalents." (An example of this is given in the next chapter.) It follows that disaffected patients, unable to represent mentally an idea linked to its emotional quality, and equally unable for the reasons outlined above to repress such presentations, must instead have recourse to the more primitive mechanisms of splitting and projective identification to protect themselves from being overwhelmed by mental suffering. The individual then ejects from consciousness the idea with its accompanying affect, instead projecting these onto the representation of another person in his internal world. A representative of this internal object is subsequently sought in the external world; in this way such people unconsciously evoke in others, by their very ways of talking and acting, the feelings that they themselves have repudiated. In fact, they frequently talk and act in the way their parents did when they were little, and often have no other means of communicating their feeling of paralysis and pain. (This maneuver has been extensively discussed in earlier writings, notably in McDougall, 1978, Chapter 7.)

In the psychoanalytic relationship this aspect of the analysand's discourse, through the confused, anxious, irritated or bored feelings it tends to arouse, often alerts and enables the analyst to feel, sometimes poignantly, the double-bind messages and the forgotten pain and distress of the small child who had to learn to deaden inner liveliness in order to survive. Clinical aspects of these problems will be dealt with in the following chapter.

CHAPTER 7

The Analyst and the Disaffected Patient

W HEN SEARCHING FOR suitable clinical examples to illustrate the propositions of the last chapter, I noticed, somewhat tardily, that the patients who came to mind had frequently had a previous analysis or had been in analysis with me for a number of years. In other words, I realized that this kind of affect problem *may have passed unnoticed* in analytic work for a number of years. The patients themselves were unaware that they suffered from an inability to recognize their emotional experiences, since these were either totally split off from consciousness or, if briefly conscious, immediately dispelled in some form of action.

One dominant feature was a conscious sense of failure, of missing the essence of what life was supposed to be, or of wondering why their personal lives, in contrast to other people's, seemed empty and boring. Frequently the initial years of analysis had been useful in overcoming a number of neurotic problems and inhibitions; however, once these were out of the way, there was laid bare a profound though nonspecific impression of dissatisfaction with life, of which the analysands had hitherto been unaware. It appeared probable that certain neurotic structures had served, among other functions, to camouflage underlying states of irrepresentable despair or anonymous anguish. The ongoing psychoanalytic process also led to my patients' discovery that they had very little *affect tolerance* and that this had been masked not only by the neurotic symptoms but more particularly by addictive behavior of the different kinds already discussed.

These patients eventually revealed a terror of their psychic reality that had in fact put them out of contact with it. Some (like Tim quoted in the next chapter) managed to eliminate from memory almost all of my interpretations and interventions as part of the disaffected armor-plating. Tim, instead of being able to give himself up to the luxury of free association, had developed an anal fortress of almost impregnable strength and thus remained unaware of any trace of transference feeling or any feelings of almost any order within his own experience.

Little Jack Horner, whose analysis I am now going to discuss, had quite a different form of defense. Instead of fighting with constipated silence or with rapid elimination of any affective arousal, he took recourse in more "oral" means of attack and defense. Far from remaining silent, he would throw out words and imprecations like so many rocks. In spite of this apparently lively form of communication, I came to learn that he too was severely disaffected in certain areas of his life.

Here is a brief excerpt from his long period of analysis with me. For some years Jack usually arrived as he put it, "deliberately 15 minutes late because this analysis is of no value." (In spite of this seeming protestation, he never once missed a session in eight years.) Prior to coming to see me Jack had had 12 years of analysis with two different male analysts. During our first two interviews, he expressed his conviction that I would be unable to understand him and therefore incompetent to help him. I said that I would take the risk if he were willing to do so, for he seemed to me a highly interesting and complex personality, with a somewhat childlike appeal; in addition, he suffered from neurotic problems that he thought should have cleared up years ago.

I shall not give an account of these long years of treatment except to illustrate the nature of the analytic relationship and the curious affect economy Jack displayed. Whenever I made a remark he would say something like, "I cannot imagine where you get your good reputation from." After two years, this plaint changed slightly: "Maybe you're able to do something for the others, but I can tell you right now, it's never going to work with me!" When I suggested that this might be a rather uncomfortable situation to find himself in, he remembered something he had heard about Doberman guard dogs. These animals apparently suffer from character problems. According to Jack, they become passionately attached to their first master and are even capable of transferring their affection to a second, but should they be unfortunate enough to find themselves saddled with a third master, they might just tear him to pieces.

Sensing the desperate person inside him, endlessly searching for the analyst (or parent) who would finally be able to help him — and whom he could hate with impunity — I said, "And I am your third analyst.'" There followed a moment of heavy silence before Jack Horner could gather his plums together again: "Really! You and your little analytic interpretations!" As can be imagined, the analysis of transference affect was no simple matter. Indeed, Jack frequently cut me off in the middle of a sentence, just as though I were not speaking at all. When I once pointed this out to him, he replied that I was there to listen to him and there was nothing he wished or needed to hear from me.

As the months went by I realized that he tended to be narcissistically wounded by my interpretations. I began to feel depressed about this apparently unfruitful analytic voyage, but with time I understood that this was the essential message, a primitive communication intended to make me feel what the distressed and misunderstood infant in Jack's inner psychic world had once felt: that communication is useless and the desire for a live affectionate relationship hopeless.

With Jack I was not a "fecal lump" destined to be evacuated, as I understood it with Tim; metaphorically, I was more like a defective breast that, consequently, deserved to be demolished. The fact that one is constantly denigrated or eliminated as imaginary feces or breast, without embodying any of the potentially valuable aspects of these part objects, is not the problem. On the contrary, these unconscious projections are the sign that something is happening in the analytic relationship. In spite of their continuing negativism, I was very attached to the two patients I am comparing at this moment; nevertheless, I frequently felt fed up with both of them. My discouragement arose from the fact that, in spite of vivid signs of suppressed feeling and underlying drama that might find expression in words, the analyses stagnated. The apparent lack of any psychic change — or indeed a negative therapeutic reaction — evokes negative countertransference feelings. A relentless attack upon the analytic setting, the relationship, or the process itself is profoundly significant and can potentially provide valuable insight into the patient's underlying personality structure and psychic survival techniques. But if its meaning holds no interest for the analysand, or if what has been understood is either forgotten or denied, then we are probably dealing with a primitive form of defense that has been marshalled to head off an impression of impending, perhaps mortal, danger at the thought of change. It is comprehensible that such analysands may also have difficulty understanding other people's affective experience — including the analyst's. The upshot is that the others become strongly "affected" instead!

The fundamental problem is of a preneurotic order. These patients act as though subject to an inexorable maternal law that questioned their right to exist in a lively and independent way. In some cases they experienced themselves as a narcissistic extension of the mother's self and therefore compelled to complete her sense of self and attend to her needs. My clinical experience has led me to the conviction that this deeply incarnated "law" was one of the first elements to develop in their sense of self and that it is transmitted, in the beginning, through the mother's gestures, voice, and ways of looking at, holding, and otherwise responding to her baby's states of excitement and its affect storms. For it is the mother alone who must decide whether to encourage or restrain her infant's spontaneity. However, it is not my intention to explore, in this chapter, the personal past, the phallic-oedipal, or pregenital

meaning independent existence

oedipal organizations of the patients in question. These issues are more clearly illustrated in other chapters. For the moment I wish to concentrate on the factors in the analytic experience that relate to the way the psychic economy functions.

In stating that the problems are preneurotic, I do not mean to suggest that neurotic symptoms and neurotic character patterns are lacking. They are clearly evident but may prevent our sensing a deeper anguish. Perhaps for this reason the analysands themselves either do not recognize the existence of their neurotic suffering or make light of it to the point of disinterest. When neurotic features are accessible to the analytic process, we frequently find that they have been kept intact to serve as an alibi for deeper and more terrifying psychic disturbances.

Jack, for example, brought to his first interview, as though offering me a gift that would entitle him to treatment, two "good" neurotic symptoms (both of which, as the reader will perceive, may be seen as having a psychosomatic dimension). Jack had managed to maintain, throughout 40 years of life and 12 years of previous analysis, a certain form of sexual impotence as well as recalcitrant insomnia that had dogged him since his adolescence. Each symptom was in part linked to hitherto unconscious homosexual fears and wishes and both disappeared within the first three years of our work together.

Jack was by no means happy about these changes. If anything, he resented this passage in his analytic voyage. "No doubt you congratulate yourself on the disappearance of my two symptoms. But nothing's really changed. It's perfectly normal to sleep at nights, and as for making love, you might as well know that as far as I'm concerned it's something like cleaning my teeth. I feel it's necessary and I often feel better afterwards. But as for *me*—I'm more unhappy than ever before. My symptom, my real symptom, is that *I don't know how to live*."

Behind the evident pathos of such a statement, we might also wonder who, in Jack's inner world, is "me." Is it the adult who now sleeps soundly? Or the man who makes love without hindrance? In a sense these experiences are not part of "him"; they are excluded from what he feels to be his true self. His "real me," as he understands it, suffers from a deep sense of deadness, for which he believes there is no cure, as though this part of him had never truly come alive. Moreover, should it threaten to do so, *it must immediately be rendered lifeless, feelingless, and therefore meaningless*.

Our analytic work up to this point led me to the disquieting recognition that Jack's former neurotic symptoms had, among other factors, served to camouflage the background scene of his internal theater; once gone, they left behind a disaffected, empty depression that left its imprint on his sleep, devoid of dreams, and on his sexual life, devoid of love. His image of his personal identity seemed rather like a faded photograph to which he nevertheless clung as a sign of psychic survival. I asked myself, "Have I become the frame in which the sepia-tinted portrait can be guaranteed a place? Jack claims that he cannot leave me in spite of his conviction that I can do nothing to bring him to life. How are we to understand this impression of inner death that freezes each vital impulse?" It is as though it were forbidden to Jack, for impalpable reasons, to enjoy life, to delight in his own experience of feeling alive in each important facet of his existence, as well as to accepting those moments of disappointment, anger, or narcissistic pain which are part of everybody's lot.

To come back to my central question: What happens to the inaccessible affect in this case? Clearly, it does not follow the economic and dynamic paths described by Freud in hysterical and obsessional structures and in the so-called actual neuroses (which today we would call states of severe affect pathology), such as depression and panic anxiety. With analysands like Jack there is, on the contrary, a serious *deficiency* of protective defenses and of effective action in the face of psychological pain, whether derived from narcissistic-libidinal or object-libidinal sources. The fear of being overwhelmed, of implosion or explosion in relationships with others, often obliges people to attack not only their perception of their emotions but also any external perceptions that might arouse affect. In the course of analysis we are sometimes the privileged observers of this radical elimination of emotionally charged events and may discover just what happens to the stifled affect in question.

Although many interesting features in the psychic structure of patients like Jack might be taken into consideration, my intention is to use a fragment from Jack's analysis simply to highlight the nature of the affective disturbance and to illustrate what occurs at moments when such analysands are out of touch with the emotional aspects of their psychic reality.

Jack Attacks External Reality

As already remarked, Jack usually arrived from 10 to 15 minutes late, proclaiming that, in any case, he was better off in the waiting room than on the couch. As a result of my drawing attention to this acting-out on numerous occasions, he eventually became curious, during the fifth year of our work, about the unconscious meaning of his unpunctual behavior and told me that he intended to come right on time to the next session. Apparently he came 10 minutes early. Due to unforeseen and unavoidable circumstances I myself was 10 minutes *late*. Given the context I found this most unfortunate, and I told him so. As he lay down on the couch, he said, "Good heavens, I couldn't care less! I was very happy there alone. The time passed quickly because I had found an interesting article to read. In fact, when you came to the door, I didn't even see you—that is, I got a vague impression that you were unusually small. Actually, I was aware that you aren't dressed with your usual elegance. Seems to me you're wearing a sort of dirty-grey thing." (I was wearing a dress of apricot-colored suede with a long white scarf which I thought was rather elegant!) "Oh yes and another thing, it's as though you didn't have any head. That's it—you looked shrunken and colorless."

In attempting to analyze the negative feelings that I suggested may have been aroused during his long wait, he deduced, as though it were an exercise in logic, that perhaps he should have had vaguely hostile feelings—but in fact he felt nothing of the kind and doubted that he would be capable of such an emotion with regard to me. From here he went on to a chain of associations that included certain screen memories from the past, as well as some pivotal fantasies we had discussed in the course of this lengthy analysis. These might be considered "reconstructed screen memories" or historical constructions that had become an integral part of our work.

At this point Jack took up one of these "memories" (that had become a certainty for him over the years) that something disastrous and irrevocable had occurred between him and his mother when he was 4 months old. His thoughts then turned to a photograph taken of him as a little boy of around 15 months, which he always referred to as "the baby sitting alone in the snow." In reality this snapshot, which he once brought to show me, showed him sitting in sunshine on a white sandy beach.

On listening to him at this particular moment in the session, my own free-floating thoughts in response to his associations went as follows: "There's Jack Horner, 'baby-alone-in-the-snow,' feeling cold and abandoned, now alone in my waiting room, but determined to know nothing about these feelings, which doubtless would have resuscitated a traumatic situation of the past." Without perceiving any link in his chain of thoughts, Jack then went on to recall a moment in our second year of work together, when he had rather suddenly expressed the wish to break off treatment. Since he had already described the tempestuous manner in which he had terminated his two previous analyses, I suggested that we should leave space to examine the reasons for his sudden decision, instead of repeating an old pattern without understanding it. From that time on Jack reproached me continually for not having grasped the supreme importance of his spontaneous wish to leave the analysis and claimed that I had permanently destroyed his chances of experiencing a true desire: "You should have known that I wouldn't have left anyhow. But no, you had to spoil everything. Now it's ruined forever. I shall never again have a spontaneous wish of my own."

Here then today was little Jack Horner, picturing himself as four months or fifteen months old, full of life, making spontaneous and meaningful gestures to the analyst-mother. However, she turns out to be an implacable, uncaring or absent mother who forces

him to accept, once and for all, that he can never aspire to personal
freedom, spontaneous desires, vitality and excitement, except at
the price of losing his mother's love and reassuring presence. His
reaction was that of a tiny child who had to attack his *perception*
of the mother whom he felt had rejected and hurt him: His mother
has no head, she has become small and colorless, a desiccated and
devitalized image from which he pulls away. But in so doing he
internalizes her, so that it is with this devitalized mother that he
now identifies in his attitude toward his own child-self. For the
infant he still feels himself to be cannot give up his mother. She is
life itself. Instead he gives up his own vitality. He would rather
freeze himself forever into the image of the "baby-alone-in-the-
snow," now playing a dual role—at one and the same time the
rambunctious child and the disapproving, unresponsive, uncom-
prehending mother. In the transference he was able to project this
particular internal mother-representation onto me.

André Green (1973), referring to psychotic modes of experiencing affect, noted that "paradoxical affectivity expresses itself in
action and in impulsive behaviour of an explosive and unexpected
kind. The link between affect and representation can be glimpsed
in the relationship between acts and hallucinatory activity. The
affect is acted out and its representation no longer obeys reality."
Green then goes on to quote Bion's view (1959) that, for certain
psychotic patients, reality as such is hated, with resulting inhibition of affective experience by the ego. At the same time, there are
destructive attacks on all psychic processes. These include attack
upon the representation or perception of the object, upon the
subject's own body, and above all, upon his own thought processes. Affects are not only infiltrated with hatred, but hated as
such.

Patients like Jack and Tim (Chapter 8) do indeed use psychotic
defense mechanisms, but they do not suffer from disordered psychotic thinking. Jack remarked on a couple of occasions that he
was an "autistic child," Tim referred to himself in our initial interview as a "schizoid individual," and Christopher (Chapter 3)
claimed that he was a "backward child in a psychotic mode." But
in each case this was the adult part of the personality observing

and commenting on the distressed and traumatized child within. In a sense it was, for each of these patients, an intellectual defense against actually *listening* to the child's messages and caring for this damaged child-part.

The countertransference difficulties that almost unavoidably arise do not reside in an inability to identify with the nursling hidden in these analysands' internal worlds. They derive instead from recognition of their utter inability to believe that they can be helped with the distress they feel. They prefer to destroy any offers of help rather than plunge once again into the traumatic experiences of infancy. Due to the lack of a caretaking, maternal introject (Krystal 1978a, 1978b), they cannot listen in a meanful way to what is occurring. This becomes painfully evident in the analytic relationship when the analyst is thrust into the role of the inadequate, incompetent, or totally absent mother with whom the analysand is still trying, in unconscious fantasy, to "settle accounts" derived from the unfinished business of childhood. Once these fantasies, and the behavior to which they give rise, become conscious and analyzable, other images of the mother become available for thinking and producing eventual psychic change. (This is particularly clear in the case of Georgette, Chapter 10.)

Over and beyond this complex projection of a maternal object the analyst also must accept being experienced as the father who has also failed in his task, namely, to protect the child from the implosive mother-image. Not only is the father believed to forbid and condemn attachment to the "breast mother," but he is also thought to offer no compensations for the renunciations that would be involved. Sometimes, as already emphasized, this lopsided oedipal organization may lead to an attempt to replace the forbidden internalization of the mother with addictive substances. The mother thereby becomes, as in perturbed infancy, *not an object of longing and libidinal wishes but purely an object of need.* The representation of the father then is invested as a person who refuses the nursling the right to become a separate individual and perhaps even to live. Thus it is Narcissus rather than Oedipus who implores us to rescue him. This also means that the analyst will be expected to support the demands and blows of the enraged child who is struggling, with the means at his disposal, for the right to exist.

From the standpoint of the countertransference our own "Narcissus" is sorely tried. We are tempted to ask ourselves: "Why should this child need so much more understanding, care, and nourishment, than the others?" (But the depleted child within *does* need more than a neurotically structured patient who has in his internal world two "good-enough" parents.) Patience is required, for we must manage to restrain and elaborate our own affective reactions while waiting for the birth of a true desire in the other; such desire will differ from an angry demand for vengeance and the expectation of total reparation. This task presents a particular hazard in that we are faced with a dimension of inner death that permeates the analytic discourse and threatens our own internal vitality. We too may fall victim to our patients' disenchantment with all their relationships, in turn disinvesting a laborious, and seemingly interminable, psychoanalytic voyage. That is, we may end up agreeing that this journey is not worth undertaking. We need to be convinced that some psychic change is possible, and that our disaffected analysands will one day have the courage to leave their thin survival lines and begin to live.

This reflection on countertransference attitudes raises another pertinent question. Why do we accept in analysis those whose aim is to resist the psychoanalytic process as though their lives were in danger—those who have an urgent though usually unconscious need to make the analysis fail through terror of the unknown world that may open up should there be any important change. To the desperate child hidden within these recalcitrant adults, change can only be for the worse. This fear gives added impetus to continual acting-out, attacks upon the psychoanalytic setting or the analytic relationship, or constant elimination of every insight enlightened by a glimmer of hope that life may become a creative adventure instead of a battlefield. The cry for help of these analysands might appear at times to express itself in a form which recalls the credo of the addict: "Please help me, but you will find out that I am stronger than you. You'll get nowhere."

The fact of the matter is that we are frequently unaware of the difficult analytic path ahead of us when we engage ourselves in such analyses. No doubt we are sometimes motivated by the narcissistic wish to succeed where others have failed! In addition, there is always a tendency to project onto a future analysand considerable potential for undertaking an analysis. We are inclined to believe that the patient will be capable of making good use of us and to convince ourselves, in the preliminary interviews, that we have perceived a positive dimension to his psychic structure. We sense that these patients are desperate for help and this takes on the air of a positive sign; no doubt we want to believe that anyone who seems seriously to seek analysis, who is aware of psychic suffering and eager to discover its causes, is analyzable. There is probably a Dr. Knock hidden inside each of us who is convinced that everyone can benefit from analysis and that every psychoanalytic voyage is worth the effort!

As far as I myself am concerned, to the extent that a potential patient reveals a wish to make discoveries about his or her unknown inner world, this evokes in me a similar desire. Even those who have already spent long years in analysis and yet wish to continue their quest call forth the wish to know more, to discover what still remains to be brought to light, as though it were a challenge to our capacity for further exploration. Perhaps the countertransference pitfall is a desire to know *too much*? Bion once remarked that an analyst is someone who prefers to read a person rather than a book.

But suppose we are fooling ourselves? What if there is no readable story in this book because the writer has never been given the words with which to begin it? Or has never dared turn the first page for fear of what he would read and reveal to himself and to us? Perhaps the beginning of the story is also the end, so that we go round in unceasing circles while trying to read a little further. However this may be, once we start on this voyage, we must assume responsibility for the mutual enterprise. Admittedly, we do this at a certain price. The analysands who paralyze our "reader-analyst" function arouse in us painful feelings of malaise. How can we give life to those who ask only that we help them keep their prison walls intact—and our emotional reactions to ourselves?

How are we to deal with the feeling of total impotence caused by our inability to render them less disaffected, less hopeless, so that they can eventually wish to leave us and to live?

Finally, what are we to do with our own feelings of despair about ourselves and our work? It is said that if one looks at anything for a long enough time, it becomes interesting. Although we are always alone in our observation of our affectless or inaccessible patients, and although we know that nobody is going to come and help us with the relationship, we at least have the possibility of sharing our disquiet, our sense of incompetence and our incomprehension. This is one of the reasons that we give papers, organize colloquiums and write books! Thus therapists and patients alike, as well as those interested laymen who are neither analysands nor analysts (and who are perhaps capable of being their own psychoanalysts), may share our clinical experience and our theoretical searchings. Even when the patients who resist the analytic process awaken in us the dread of an interminable analytic experience, we may feel grateful to them for having opened before us a field of research as yet unsown.

As Jack Horner once said to me, after eight years of searching for further glimpses of his inner world, "I have neutralized you completely. It doesn't matter what you do or say; you will never get anywhere with me." When I asked his permission to use the vignette quoted above and to mention his feelings of hopelessness about our work he replied, "Why not? My analysis is utterly useless to me, but I expect you'll manage to make a little article out of it!"

CHAPTER 8

The Reasons of the Heart

BLAISE PASCAL, THE French philosopher and physicist, in his celebrated *Pensées* published as long ago as 1670, proclaimed that: "Le coeur a ses raisons que la raison ne connaît point." If poets, lovers and mystics have always known that "the heart hath reasons that reason knoweth not," it is perhaps because they intuitively sense that the heart is the essential organ of affect, the metaphor of love, grief, and nostalgia, as well as of hatred, rage, and violence. The fragment of analysis that follows recounts the analytic story of a man whose childhood ideal was to be "heartless," so that he might feel neither physical nor mental pain. Amid traumatic circumstances, into the mind of this courageous little boy had been instilled an ideal of emotional invulnerability. At least this was how the child of yesteryear interpreted his mother's admonitions. In the light of our psychoanalytic voyage, which lasted some six years, it does seem probable that the bereaved mother, unable to hold onto and think through her own emotional pain, had promulgated for her children a hidden law that demanded absolute mastery of feelings under all conditions. Fear, tears, anger, or any other display of emotion ran the risk of incurring her displeasure and worse still, the threat of losing her love. While of her love there was no doubt, it too was not to be mentioned.

Mid-thirties, round-rimmed glasses, a round-necked sweater with blue jeans — Tim wore the typical air of a serious but youthful professor. He wished to continue an analysis to which he had put an end two years earlier. "I spent five years with this analyst. He helped me to feel more sure of myself, to think more clearly, to dress better . . . but somehow none of my fundamental problems changed. I still feel perpetually empty . . . and out of touch with others." As long as he could remember it had always been this way.

To all outward appearances, Tim was living a peaceful and successful life. However, there had been two career changes and his present position as teacher in a local university had now lost interest for him. Although attached to his wife and daughters, he claimed that he felt nothing of the pleasure they seemed to derive from everyday living. He sometimes had difficulty in believing that they were not playacting. He made love with his wife frequently and without difficulty but his sexual life held little interest for him since he rarely experienced any sensation of pleasure in lovemaking. At the same time he did not appear to regard this lack of pleasure as a symptom. In his work milieu the interest that several women had shown toward him aroused neither desire nor daydreams.

Of his childhood Tim selected the sparsest of details for my information. His father died unexpectedly when he was seven and no other man ever took his place in the household. By dint of hard work Tim's mother raised Tim and his two elder sisters singlehandedly. "I remember the day of my father's death very well," said Tim, "but I don't recall being deeply affected. I never cried. I was staying with relatives for a few days' vacation when it happened. The day before, I'd had an unaccountable bowel accident and was quite ashamed for such a thing hadn't happened to me in a long while. Then the next day my aunt said she had some sad news about my father. My first thought was that he'd been put in prison.

But when she told me he was dead I was convinced that it was my fault—because of the bowel accident in my pants. As though I'd killed him that way."

When I asked Tim if he had memories of his father before his death, he replied, "Oh yes. He was a 'bon vivant'." In French this phrase refers to someone who is jovial, good-humored and interested in the earthy things of life. But the literal meaning is "good and alive"—a somewhat paradoxical way of describing a dead father! I asked myself whether seven-year-old Tim had buried all his own vitality and joie de vivre with his "good and alive" father. To the arid portrait he offered of himself Tim added that, as far back as he could remember, not only had he never cried but he had never had a dream. There emanated from him an air of despair and inner death that went beyond sadness and tears, and that seemed to have rendered him incapable of experiencing pleasure in any single aspect of his life. "I suppose you'd call me a schizoid kind of person," he concluded ruefully.

I asked Tim what he wished to obtain from the continuation of his analysis. "Maybe I have to deal with much deeper things than my father's death. I talked a lot about that in my first analysis. I recalled quite vividly wanting to take his place with my mother and being so disappointed when she wouldn't let me sleep in her bed. But I've no early memories at all. That's why I thought a woman analyst might help me to delve deeper." After a short silence he added, "It's as though I'm searching for a lost part of myself." I believe this phrase was decisive in my acceptance of Tim as a future patient. He declared that he was eager to begin his analytic adventure but did not mind waiting for a year or so until I had a place for him.

When our work finally began some 18 months later, to my surprise Tim arrived 15 to 20 minutes late for every session. He would then lie down in silence for a further 10 minutes during which time he would take off and replace his glasses, as though debating whether or not to tell me what he could see. Soon he began to miss sessions for no ostensible reason. Whenever I announced a vacation break he would disappear from the analytic scene a week before my departure. My interpretations of his lateness, prolonged silence, and frequent absences led nowhere. He agreed intellectually that these might reflect anxiety or hostility about our relationship or an attack on the analytic process itself and that he might therefore wish to put some distance between us. "That's an interesting idea," he would comment, "but I don't feel anything." He also accepted the interpretation that no doubt he needed to be in control of experiences of separation, although he insisted that these "interesting ideas," which evoked no emotion in him, were purely logical deductions. Predictably, therefore, they brought no psychic change in their wake and were subsequently forgotten.

To Tim's pitifully small harvest of childhood memories, in particular that of his father spreading gaiety around the house, or enjoying a drink with his pals (despite his wife's disapproval), was added a never-forgotten scene in which his father killed the family cat by hitting it on the head with an axe. This cruel act, Tim alleged, was his mother's fault since she constantly complained of the cat's messy behavior. The suggestion that Tim might have feared his father's reaction to little boys with messy behavior awakened no echos in his mind. Nor did he accept any connection between this scene and his own childhood fantasy of having killed his father by fecal expulsion. Once when I recalled this detail he did, however, bring forth one more childhood memory—of a long period of insomnia during which he would tiptoe about the house, afraid that his state of tension might bring down the walls and kill his mother and his sisters! These different recollections evoked for me the image of a little boy terrified by his own violence and his omnipotent power to bring death to those he loved. We nicknamed this fantasy-killer, now totally imprisoned inside Tim's adult personality, his "King Kong" self, but it rapidly became one more lost part. Tim remained literally "unaffected" by his memories as well as by my interpretations of their possible underlying significance. I alone was affected. The emotions that might have been thought to accompany such childhood recollections appeared entirely absent in Tim and could be attached neither to the transference nor to the figures of the past. Tim declared he had no strong feelings about anything, and in fact did not believe that as a child he had been particularly anxious, violent, or unhappy. As for our relationship, he regretted that he found no trace of either positive or negative feelings toward me; he was equally unaware of any marked emotions concerning other people in his life. Rather, their affective reactions to events and to other people appeared to him to be incomprehensible. When people showed pleasure over accomplishments or expressed concern in the face of misfortune, Tim had difficulty believing that these emotions were genuine.

One day, as he continued complaining that life was meaningless, I told him that everything he had recounted thus far made me keenly aware of the existence of a sad and embittered little boy within him who had buried the lively part of himself with his dead father and who doubted, therefore, whether his existence could be meaningful to others. He seemed to take it for granted that his wife, his mother, and his analyst were indifferent to the survival of this unhappy child. After a stunned silence Tim replied, "This idea — that somehow I don't exist for other people — affects me so deeply I'm almost unable to breathe." He sounded as though he were on the verge of tears and remained silent, breathing heavily, until the end of the session. I eagerly awaited the next analytic hour. After his usual mute 10 minutes, Tim began, "I'm tired of this analysis and your eternal silence. Nothing ever happens since you never say a word. I should have gone to a Kleinian!" All trace of the previous session had vanished! Later, I was able to understand that at the very moment Tim began to have trouble breathing, he was already expelling from his mind and body the memory of my words along with their psychological and physical repercussions — that is, their affective impact.

On another occasion, this fortress of emotional invulnerability, which had weathered the attacks of time as well as my interpretations, once more yielded slightly. During a session in which Tim again complained of feeling lifeless and useless, I said that it must have been difficult for a little boy of seven suddenly to find himself the man of the household without any father to tell him how to be a man. To my surprise, and Tim's intense embarrassment, he burst into tears — his first tears, in many long years, so far as he could remember. During the session he accepted the proposition that he had reacted not only with feelings of grief and guilt, but also with an impression of narcissistic damage when his beloved and lively father died, leaving him feeling lifeless and useless. Several days later when I referred again to the little bereaved boy, Tim could scarcely remember that he had cried and had totally forgotten the content of the session! This was to become a repeated pattern, as though any thoughts capable of reactivating emotion had to be swiftly evacuated from consciousness. Tim's unconscious psychic pattern of cutting any link to ideas charged with affect, whether pleasureable or painful, was the most striking feature of his mode of mental functioning.

Here we see at work once again the signs of psychic deprivation discussed in Chapter 3, in which both the mental representation and its accompanying affect are rapidly expelled from the mind without any sign or symptom arising as a substitute. We must recall that such psychic foreclosure, as already discussed at length in Chapter 6, is of a different order from that associated with repression or denial and approximates a process associated with psychosis. Previous clinical experience had led me to the conclusion that these archaic forms of defense against mental pain, in which splitting and projection had to do duty for repression, were frequently connected with early psychic trauma. I had also discovered in my practice that this specific way of psychic functioning was often associated with addictive proclivities, as well as with severe psychosomatic manifestations. But these did not appear to be Tim's problems. Only later did I realize that I should have paid more attention to these disquieting signs and drawn Tim's attention to his way of attacking any thought or event capable of arousing emotion.

With no hint of the tragedy to come, I nevertheless felt discouraged and oppressed by this analysis. Faced with Tim's strangely affectless way of experiencing both the present and the past, I sought to make longer interventions in an effort to fill up the empty, deathlike silence that lay behind Tim's words and appeared to invade his inner universe. At the same time I was also struggling to combat the temptation to fall into "dead silence" myself. I surmised at this early stage of our work together that behind Tim's traumatic experience of losing his father in childhood lay more primitive psychic distress in infancy, which had doubtless complicated the already difficult task that mourning presents for small children. Had not Tim himself proclaimed in our initial meeting that he was seeking insight into primitive aspects of his relationship to his mother? Yet he seemed unable to provide any clues as to what these might be. Without dreams, fantasies or free associations to help us, we both became aware of a feeling of stalemate.

Attempting to cooperate in our analytic quest, Tim went so far as to ask his mother whether any unusual events had marked his early childhood. She replied that the war, coupled with his father's death, had made life hard for the little family and added, to Tim's astonishment, that as a very little boy he had been extremely disobedient and unruly. She had had to work hard to get him to comply with her standards for good behavior. All trace of these early oppositional years had vanished from Tim's mind. As long as he could remember he had always been reserved, calm, and detached. We conjectured that the change may have been wrought following his father's death.

By the end of our second year of work Tim no longer arrived late or missed sessions. With regard to his precipitate departures before each vacation, he accepted the interpretation that he may have felt an urge to control separation experiences of this kind, since his father had died while he was on vacation. He admitted that the thought had sometimes occurred to him that I might die during a holiday break, thus leaving him in the lurch. At other times he also gave me the role of his mother, "who invariably made all the decisions without consulting anyone." In consequence therefore, he felt obliged to refuse to abide by the dates decided by me. This year he announced his attention of staying right till the last session before the summer break.

As the summer approached, a new theme appeared in Tim's associations. The thought returned with insistence that he would soon be 40 years old. When I asked what this meant to him he replied, "Well, when I was young I always said that I wouldn't live beyond 40, that after 40 one was nothing but a leftover." Since Tim seemed unable to associate any further to this idea, it occurred to me (somewhat tardily, I admit) to ask him at what age his father had died. Tim searched for a while in his memory. "Let's see . . . I think he died in the summer. Yes! As a matter of fact he was in his fortieth year." My attempts to get Tim to explore fantasies about his own death, a possible childhood wish to join his father, feelings of guilt about his father's death and about his having survived his father, and so on, led nowhere. Tim was unable to try such ideas out for possible clues and proclaimed that he was unaware of any particular emotions connected with these thoughts.

I come now to the most traumatic part of Tim's and my analytic adventure. One week before my vacation was to begin, Tim's wife phoned me at the time of his session to tell me that during the night Tim had had a myocardial infarct. She assured me he was out of danger but would probably be hospitalized for some time. In reply to a question on my part, she said that Tim had not had the slightest inkling of any cardiac pathology, although he smoked incessantly and was frequently out of breath. I asked for the hospital address before saying goodbye and sank into my chair with a feeling of having myself suffered a traumatic shock.

During the time of Tim's session (which had now become an analytic session with myself) I tried to gather together my ideas about him, to take notes — and to brush away some tears. I had been unaware of Tim's excessive smoking and thought back upon the many occasions in which he had had fantasies of bringing dirt, cigarette butts, or dog droppings into my room, and of a solicitous remark, "I hope I'm not poisoning your lungs." I had interpreted these as childhood fantasies of amorously entering my body with his feces, as well as their aggressive counterpart, of visiting upon me the fate of his father whom, in Tim's childhood fantasy, he had killed by his sudden expulsion of feces. Had Tim given me, in these fantasies, the death he almost visited upon himself? While expressing concern for my lungs, in reality he had been "poisoning" his own, as though he could only care for himself through caring for me.

In thinking back over my countertransference reactions to his sessions, I realized that I had often experienced a compelling need to intervene, to be lively in his place, while concomitantly feeling paralyzed by his associations. Many a time I had produced fantasies in his place, as well as picking up the threads of past sessions which he invariably let drop. Was he settling accounts with an archaic image of his mother whom he believed incapable of "hearing" him? of understanding his needs? of giving him the right to his own identity? of wanting him to live? Or was he punishing himself for his inability to keep his father alive? With Tim's capacity to eliminate from memory every analytic interaction that caught his interest or stirred him emotionally, I had also played the role of his memory system with regard to thoughts and feelings.

Still very distraught, I decided to write to Tim expressing my concern and adding that, when he was sufficiently well to return, we would have many "vital issues" to discuss. After some deliberation I began the letter: "Dear Tim." The use of first names in French professional relationships is extremely rare, but I could not bring myself to address him, conventionally, as "Cher Monsieur." To my surprise I received a letter by return mail in which he wrote, "When I saw the words 'Dear Tim' at the beginning of your letter it was as though I possessed this name for the very first time in my life." This phrase strengthened my conviction that Tim had indeed grown up uncertain of his right to exist or at least to be fully alive and enjoy all aspects of what adult life may offer.

I reformulated the old questions: Was Tim seeking to settle accounts with an archaic mother figure who heard nothing, neither his needs nor his desires? Who did not wish him to live? Was he therefore seeking an erotic fusion with his "good-and-alive" father in the tomb? Then the uneasy question that returned insistently to my mind: Had Tim left in my keeping his will to live, and with it the wish that I would dream, daydream, and desire for him? Perhaps this allowed his own deathlike drive and unrepresentable depression to continue their insidious work. What had I failed to hear? The violence of his own aggression? His death wishes toward me? Toward himself?

Further queries without answers surged in upon me. Perhaps I had been too much the mother trying to protect the mourning child stifled within his imprisoning adult self. As a result had I assumed too little the role of a live father, capable of imposing on his son the recognition of his anger and hatred and their secret fantasy-aims? Whatever the answers to these myriad questions might be, it seemed to me they must refer to something vitally important that I had not as yet perceived—for even when I talked at length Tim claimed that I had said nothing!

The few answers I have been able to find to these questions, meager though they are, were the fruit of five years of construction and reconstruction. Tim did learn to dream, to daydream, and to cry. The slow process by which these acquisitions came into being, as well as the underlying significance of Tim's bitter struggle during four years to give up smoking (which for him had now become a serious health hazard), is recounted in the next chapter.

CHAPTER 9

The Grief That Has
No Vent in Tears

SOME MONTHS LATER Tim returned to analysis. Before recommencing our analytic work we sat down to discuss all that had happened and what lessons might be drawn for our future work. For the first time Tim seemed genuinely interested in studying his mode of mental functioning. I emphasized the two psychological factors that seemed to me potentially life-threatening: his way of reacting when faced with thoughts and events that stirred up deep emotions and his hitherto hidden dependence on cigarette smoking.

Tim said he was aware that he appeared to suffer from some inability to grasp his feelings and that he tended to pulverize any trace of strong emotion that threatened to invade him. He wondered, as I did, whether this way of treating his affective life might have contributed to his cardiac condition—particularly since the specialists indicated that his cardiopathology had probably been building up for a number of years. I said we should not neglect to examine our analytic relationship and the effects of the analytic

129

process itself, since both might have tended to increase emotional arousal in various directions that he did not recognize. Tim agreed that this deserved reflection and that he hoped to become more aware of his affective reactions both in the analytic experience and in his relationships in the external world. However, he expressed doubt about his capacity to change in this area of his psychic life. Obviously, such a strong defense of invulnerability would not have been built up gratuitously, and we came later to discover that the thought of such change was threatening to him.

We then discussed the warning, pronounced by his doctors, of the danger in continuing to smoke. Again Tim seemed dubious about being able to give up smoking but agreed that we might learn something about his psychological need to smoke so heavily. He accepted my hypothesis that smoking might be one of his ways of dispersing feelings rather than becoming aware of them and thinking about them—as though creating a "smoke screen" between himself and that part of his psychic reality that registered affective experience.

Although there were many more intriguing facets to Tim's ensuing analysis—his oedipal preoccupations, his primitive sexual longings, his difficulty in exploring fantasies of extreme violence, his fragile narcissistic image and so on—I shall limit myself to discussing the two important aspects indicated above, namely his disaffected mode of mental functioning and his tobacco addiction, both of which now appeared as potential dangers to life itself.

The months went by, the years also, and Tim slowly became better acquainted with the fundamental problem of his inability to recognize the full range of his feelings and the highly important moments in his life. At one session he said in desperation, "I simply don't know what an emotion really is. Wait a minute—I recognize one—that time when I cried here. You know I'd do anything in the world to avoid that and yet, afterwards, it made me feel more real." He went on to proclaim, "I know . . . there are two emotions, sadness and joy! I guess that's the lot?" It was bewildering to imagine that Tim might be totally unaware of moments of rage, anxiety, love, guilt, nostalgia, and the like—or, if aware, unable to recognize and name these emotions accurately, and therefore unable to think about the events associated with them. Small wonder he had worn his heart to shreds, since his mind refused to register and deal with the larger part of his psychic reality, other than sending primitive messages that could only find expression in a regressive form of somatic discharge. There was also little doubt that Tim clung to his chain-smoking (which continued unabated in spite of the dire warnings of his doctors) as perhaps his only means of facing and overcoming emotionally charged experiences. During the session in question, knowing how wary Tim was of being swamped by overwhelming affect, I limited myself to the remark that sadness and joy were valuable psychic possessions. Tim muttered, "Yes . . . possessions . . . they're part of me."

To my delight as well as Tim's, at the next session he had not lost these new insights. "When I left here I felt very moved and, once I was in my car, my eyes filled up with tears. I said to myself that I must grab hold of the feeling, and it suddenly burst upon me. Incredible! My analyst's concerned about me; she worries about my lack of emotion." Later, on the way home, tears came once again to his eyes and this time he said, "But why is it she and not my mother who had to tell me that it is good to feel things?"

After joy and sadness the first feelings and fantasies to come to light in a meaningful way were strongly impregnated with violence, and we both came to recognize that Tim not only was afraid of his own violence but also feared that the environment (including his analyst) might not be able to cope with his upsurge of destructiveness. As his way of recounting present and past events slowly became linked to the affective experience associated with these, Tim began to feel more alive and more confident of his capacity to communicate with himself as well as with me and with others. Yet every so often these changes frightened him and the old defenses against strong affective experience would return. At these times he would claim that he was simply in better control of his emotions than most other people and therefore more adequately equipped to deal with emergencies such as road accidents and other catastrophes, where his apparent cool-headedness stood him in good stead. We replayed these inner scenarios a number of times. I would say things like, "This is Professor L, the eternally cool grown-up speaking. But what about little Tim who might need to scream with fear or shout with rage?"

On one occasion, when I asked Tim with whom this very grown-up controlled adult was identifying himself, he remembered his mother's forbidding him to cry at the time of his father's death. Tim wept throughout this session and was able, for the first time, to begin to comfort the bereaved child within him. Other forgotten memories in the same vein then came to light — such as his recalling the day his mother struck his older sister because she trembled during a bombing attack. One more brick would seem to have been added at that moment to Tim's alexithymic and disaffected fortress, in order to ensure that his emotional self would not emerge. Never would he be caught trembling like a girl!

It slowly became evident that Tim had also understood the following message: "If you are lively and freely express your feelings (as your father did), you'll die." After all, his unemotional mother had lived. Then, too, there was the possibility that Tim, in identifying with the supposed desire of his mother, had found a way of joining her, of being one with her and being loved by her.

Around the same time remembered fantasies of latency were also brought onto the analytic stage. "I've been caught by the Gestapo, but I do not say a word and show no trace of fear, pain or anger right up until I am tortured to death." Such stories, Tim remembered, brought him immense pleasure and a feeling of assurance.

Tim still did not dream but daydreams began to burst spontaneously and unexpectedly into his mind, as though coming from another world, a potential dream world. "I'm locked in a padded cell and my wife is locked in another nearby. I realize with horror that we are in a psychiatric hospital and that the director has made a false diagnosis. In fact he's crazy, and this means we shall remain in solitary confinement until the end of time." We analyzed such reveries as though they were dreams. During this session Tim gave many associations to the daydream, which led him to say that his mother's evident terror of any display of emotion on the part of her children had made him feel as though he were "imprisoned in her mind." His associations to the fantasy of being separated for life from his wife led Tim to tell me for the first time that his mother had deeply disapproved of his choice of a mate and had never been really friendly to her. He then recalled that when he was very small his mother would lock him in a dark cupboard when he was naughty, but he could not remember what misdeeds had merited this punishment. He also thought that my consultation room might be another cell into which he was locked for life.

I interpreted that the mad "director," following his associations, seemed to represent both his mother who locked him in the cupboard (and away from his wife) and myself, adding that I might well have seemed mad to him when I thought he could safely be let out of his "padded cell" and experience his fantasies and feelings of violence without danger. To this Tim replied, "Yes I feel that for two years I fled continually from you, and yet it was you who showed me that there was a way out of my locked-in state."

In the weeks that followed the fantasy of the mad director, Tim sought to refind his childhood recollections of his mother and reconstruct the relationship between them. From his scanty memories he slowly brought to light a portrait of a woman who was terrified of any display of emotion on the part of her children and who even forbade spontaneous gestures and other mute signs of affect on their behalf. His thoughts continually returned to the punishment cupboard of his early childhood, which led me to say that he identified with the punitive aspect of his mother and was now his own jailer, treating his emotional states as misdemeanors.

Tim became convinced that the disobedience and unruliness of which his mother had spoken and for which, no doubt, he was locked in the cupboard were so many desperate attempts to combat his mother's emotional stifling and attempts to control all signs of liveliness on his part—up until the fateful day when his father suddenly died. Tim now had incontrovertible proof that his mother (as he had interpreted her as a little boy) was right! Feelings and fantasies could kill! His childhood fantasy of having killed his father through fecal expulsion now began to make sense. Emotional unruliness, like a mass of murderous feces, could cause either his or his father's death. And so he became the silent, reserved, "schizoid" little boy, still dominating the adult who came to analysis, many years later, seeking a lost part of himself. This at least was our reconstruction of Tim's inner drama as it may have been around the time of his father's death. This led to his ability to mourn his lost father and to allow awareness of feelings to re-enter his adult life.

In trying to better understand his early relationship with his mother, Tim recaptured an overall impression that he had always sought to *protect* himself from her, not only because he felt that she paralyzed him but also as though she were a danger to his very life. "I couldn't even take her milk when I was born" he recounted at one session. "My uncle, who lived with us when I was little, told me that when I was a baby I had to be weaned early because of this refusal and afterwards I still refused the bottle if it was my mother who gave it to me. I could be fed only by this young uncle or by my father." Whatever the truth of these memories may have been, it was clear that Tim lived with an internal mother whom he had to reject.

TIM'S ADDICTION

Tim's early failure to introject an image of a caretaking mother with whom he could eventually identify, thus becoming a protective mother toward his own child-self, brings us to his addictive problem. His unending struggle to give up smoking, which he now accepted, to no avail, as a life-threatening addiction, became linked in various ways to his early relationship with his mother. In a sense, Tim compensated for his lack of identification to a caretaking maternal introject, with the capacity to self-soothe and to contain emotional arousal, by continually smoking as his chief means of reducing tension. He would cut down on the quantity of cigarettes or stop altogether, sometimes for up to 48 hours, only to start again when he had to face a new day. At these times, prodded by constant encouragement on my part, Tim was frequently able to uncover highly charged thoughts that he wished to elude at the moment when he believed he could no longer hold out against the need to smoke. During this period he also discovered the fragility of his affect tolerance.

These attempts on both our parts to understand his psychic economy in this respect, while essential to Tim's understanding of his addiction, were of course insufficient to produce any enduring psychic change. I also furnished many interpretations of a more dynamic order during these four years, drawn from his own associations, particularly when he strongly felt the urge to smoke during sessions. (I do not permit patients to smoke during sessions but invite them to tell me when and why they would like to do so.) On one occasion, while trying to understand the part of himself that wished for death, Tim was particularly moved when I suggested that he might have a hidden fantasy of joining his dead father.

At other times we also tracked down the many "inner people" that he might wish to stifle to death in this way (including his analyst because of her constant attempts to increase their common understanding of his suicidal behavior). However, none of my interpretations and interventions managed to unlock this particular psychic stronghold. At times I felt depressed and defeated by Tim, as though he wished us both to stifle in this cloud of smoke.

The Heart that Weeps

To illustrate the last phase of Tim's analysis with me I shall quote rather fully from a session in our sixth year of work. Tim begins by recounting his latest troubles with his automobile—a recurring theme in his analytic discourse.

TIM Of course I'd forgotten the oil again. . . . I knew it was jerking a bit but I took no notice. Now it's back in the garage.

JM Maybe we look after our cars in the same way that we treat ourselves? Some people lavish care and concern on their automobiles, but you give me the feeling that you ignore your car's coughs and splutters as though you were bent on driving it to its death.

TIM You know, I haven't liked to tell you, but I'm now back to smoking two packs a day, just like before the infarct.

JM As though you were playing Russian roulette with your life?
TIM Yeah! And yet I feel that all that is required to stop me is some
    quite small event.

During this time I sensed my mounting irritation at the thought of
all my fruitless attempts during four years to understand or effec-
tively interpret the underlying significance of Tim's suicidal behavior. I heard myself say, in response to his "waiting for some quite
small event":

JM Another infarct perhaps?
TIM Guess you're right — just waiting for the second one.

A rapid piece of self-analysis on the source of my irritation and my
consequent refusal at this moment to be more empathic led me to
feel intuitively that Tim was appealing to me through his provoca-
tive remarks, something like a three-year-old who sometimes
knocks the soup off the table "just to see if they really love him."
In consequence I had slapped him! This insight led me to a different kind of intervention.

JM Actually, I think you're waiting for something other than
    death. Is an event that could make life seem worthwhile so
    small an issue? What kind of 'small event' can you imagine?
TIM (after a long pause) Well . . . something like your remark just
    now about my playing Russian roulette with my life. That
    brought a lump to my throat — as though you feel that what is
    happening to me is serious.
JM As though your life might matter to me?
TIM Exactly! Then I could take it seriously too. (another long
    pause) You know, my wife and daughters are well aware that
    I'm back to smoking two packs a day and they do nothing
    about it.
JM It's up to *them* to do something about it? Isn't this an old
    scenario of yours that sets out to prove that nobody cares
    whether you live or die, so there's no point in *your* caring? If
    you go headlong to your death it's their fault not yours? It

seems you take your wife's inability to stop you from smoking as a proof that she wants you to die.

TIM That's absolutely true! I do think that — and it's crazy. I know only too well how much she loves me and how upset she is that I don't stop.

JM In other words, it's someone inside yourself who doesn't care a damn about your life?

TIM Who is this person? My mother was always very concerned when we fell ill. Of course, she did nothing to stop my father from dying.

JM How's that again? (Tim had never before expressed such an idea.)

TIM Well, she knew how bad his asthma was, and that if he drank and smoked as much as he did it would eventually be fatal for him.

JM Your father was also a heavy smoker?

TIM Oh yes! Terrific!

JM And it was up to your mother to stop him?

TIM I stop my wife each time she seems inclined to start again.

JM So once more you will do for another what you refuse to do for yourself?

TIM Funny, you've showed me that a number of times and I keep forgetting. What is it I refuse in there?

JM Seems to me you refuse to be a reasonably good mother to yourself. As though you were still expecting *her* to come and take care of you? Maybe you use the cigarette as a stand-in, a sort of substitute mother who will soothe your troubles away while waiting.

TIM Maybe I didn't trust her. Wait! I remember just after my father died that I believed she had killed him with a knife. And that my two sisters knew about it too. Funny, I'd forgotten all about that.

JM So the women were all killers and you could also reassure your-self that it wasn't you who had killed your father with your angry feces?

TIM Yes . . . and that way I knew he hadn't abandoned me either!

JM Perhaps this was a way of keeping a good relationship with him inside you. And then he wasn't responsible for anything, not even his overdrinking and oversmoking?

TIM You once said I wanted to smoke myself to death so I could join my father. That's something my mother couldn't hear. I was not supposed to care that he was dead.

JM There was a time when I couldn't hear it either. Neither of us could "hear" what your mother's inner distress meant to you — that she herself could not withstand or talk about strong feelings. What you needed to hear was that it was fine to love your father and to cry when he died, but that she still had you and she wanted you to *live*. Somehow she was not able to convey this.

For reasons connected with a convention he had to attend, Tim did not return until a week later. He said he had been overwhelmed because so much had happened during the last session — and then added that since that day he had not felt the need to smoke a single cigarette. (In fact, Tim did not smoke again during the rest of his analysis with me.)

Coupled with external circumstances, this turning point, which bore witness to a considerable change in Tim's way of mental functioning, led him to envisage the termination of our work together within the next few months. I felt rather torn between the wish to let Tim go so as to avoid making him feel like a helpless child unable to care for himself, and the contrary wish to analyze his projected departure as an acting-out, a sidestepping of many other difficult aspects of his inner life that still required exploration. I also felt reticent about holding him back, since he had, after all, suffered a myocardial infarct during our work together! I felt obliged to ask myself to what extent this might have been avoided had I been able to better understand him more rapidly. Did he have to pass so close to the shadow of death in order to make a genuine beginning in analysis? Might another analyst have avoided this catastrophe?

Tim himself agreed that there were many factors still to be analyzed and assured me that he would certainly continue with analysis at a more propitious time in his life — perhaps with a man. Here again I was reticent about interpreting his possible wish to take flight from transference fantasies with a woman analyst, fearing that in so doing I might well be re-enacting the drama with his mother, who was experienced as preventing him from loving his father and from mourning his death. Would I now be seen as preventing him from finding a father substitute with whom all his hidden conflicts could be worked out in new analytic situation? Since there was also the question of an important career change, my overall feeling was that maybe Tim needed to continue in the future with a truly "good-and-alive" father figure in the form of a male analyst.

We set a date for the termination which in anticipation often brought tears to Tim's eyes. Our final separation was quite moving. I was in the presence of a Tim who bore little resemblance to the apparently feelingless, "schizoid" child who had come seeking a lost part of himself. In spite of his statement that he felt he was re-experiencing a traumatic loss with the termination of his analytic work, he believed he could now leave the deathlike dimension behind him and carry away live internal parents who wished for his survival and his happiness. Toward the end of our last session he said, "You know, I only now realize that if my poor mother had been able to cry for my father's death and had let us cry together and share our grief, I might not have needed the infarct!"

After his departure I continued to question my work with Tim and the role that his heart, which had become such an important character on the psychoanalytic stage, had played in enabling him to begin his voyage into his inner psychic world and to accomplish the work of mourning that had been left so long in abeyance. There came to my mind words written over a hundred years ago, attributed to London's famous nineteenth century anatomist, Henry Maudsley: "The sorrow that has no vent in tears makes other organs weep."

CHAPTER 10

One Body for Two

I WISH TO INTRODUCE the story of a patient whose psychosomatic vulnerability was extreme, yet her mental world and way of functioning was in marked contrast to that of Tim whose analytic adventure was recounted in the preceding chapters.

This young woman suffered from an alarming array of psychosomatic maladies, many of which had been with her since early childhood. However, her extensive somatic pathology was in no way the motive for her consulting an analyst. On the contrary she seemed serenely unconcerned by her state of constant ill-health, as we shall see.

When I asked my patient, already in the ninth year of analysis, for permission to use this small fragment of her analytic adventure as a chapter in the present book, I also asked her what name she would wish me to give her. She devoted several days' thought to this choice and finally announced, "I would like to be called Georgette." Spontaneously, she offered a number of reasons for her choice, mostly having to do with positive transference elements, such as the thought that St. George was the patron saint of England. I told her I thought the legend of her inner theater, as it had come to be constructed on the analytic stage, might well read "Saint Georgette and the Dragon." She laughed and said this reminded her of one of my interventions in the second year of our work together. "I think it was the most shattering thing I had ever heard about myself. You said I seemed determined to prove to you that in every way I was a saint!" By now we both knew that the saintly little Georgette concealed a nestful of dragons in her inner psychic theater: First and foremost the dragon-like aspects of her mother, rather more slowly of myself and (in small segments) a dragon-father appeared on the analytic stage. Last, and most important of all, was the revelation of Georgette's own dragon-self, ready to slay, with burning anger and resentment, all those whom she felt had stood in her way, taken her place, leaving her feeling damaged and depleted. Until her analysis she had no knowledge of this deep fund of hatred; indeed, she had spent her life trying to be saintly, and to hurt no one; furthermore, she had engaged in a healing profession. Thus she was able to maintain an acceptable narcissistic image of herself. Meanwhile her body spat fire through almost every bodily zone and function.

It took much analytic work to discover that, paradoxically, when Georgette was most besieged with physical pain, this brought in its wake a feeling of comfort and relief from mental suffering. As time went on we came to understand that it was reassuring to her to be ill, for then she had the confirmation that her body was indeed her own, that it had limits, that it was alive, and that she herself was a separate individual who was in no danger of losing her sense of subjective identity. While these were not the causes of her illnesses, they were, so to speak, *secondary* benefits. But more than that. We also came slowly to understand that her somatic explosions were also a mute communication of thoughts and feelings that had never achieved symbolic psychic representation. They were an expression of extremely primitive but wordless libidinal longings of an archaic sexual nature whose aim was total fusion with the other. Coupled with these were other primitive fears and

wishes linked to unacknowledged narcissistic rage and mortification; to these, her many illnesses were a mute testimony.

It is the unfolding of this particular material, during our seventh
year of work, that I wish to present in this chapter. But first I must
go back to my original encounter with Georgette.

I opened the door to a slim pretty woman in her early thirties,
dressed in a thick tweed skirt, a grayish-brown pullover and flat-
heeled shoes. I had the impression that she was trying to disguise
her rather delicate feminine build and appearance. Georgette sat
down nervously in one corner of the large armchair, as though she
were going to share it with one or two others — or as though she
wished to appear inconspicuous.

GEORGETTE I need help very badly. Everything makes me anxious.
    I'm depressed much of the time. I suffer terribly whenever my
    husband goes away on business. (She fell silent, as though what
    she wished to communicate were too difficult to put into
    words.)
JM Has it been like this for some time?
G All my life. And just like now I had to hide it from everybody.
    When I was little I saw signs of death everywhere and I had to
    do magical things to keep different parts of my body from
    falling apart. I was very afraid of God . . . that he would take
    me away. I used to pray to the devil to protect me against him.

We already see that Georgette was a fanciful and indeed independent little child who apparently learned early on to protect
herself in childlike ways from impending dangers. ("Was there no
one else to whom she could turn?" I asked myself.) Georgette went
on to describe five years of a previous analysis with a man, which
had enabled her to finish her studies successfully, so that she was
now beginning practice as a pediatrician. In addition, she had
broken out of an unhappy and indeed frightening marriage which
she claimed had been imposed upon her by her mother. Her analytic exploration had made it possible for her to choose a more
compatible mate. She was now happily married and had two
children.

G But in all those years of analysis I never once spoke about anything sexual or anything to do with my body.

In recounting this Georgette's eyes remained fixed on the ground. When she dared to look at me her eyes darted anxiously around my consulting room.

G I thought it might be easier to talk to a woman. Also I once read something you had written which gave me the feeling that you would accept my being very ill psychologically. Everyone believes I'm a capable mother, wife, doctor . . . but I'm frequently crazy and I have to be careful to hide it.

I asked myself whether Georgette thought it was "crazy" to have sexual thoughts and wishes.

JM Can you tell me more about this crazy part of yourself?
G Well, I can't stop thinking about my mother. When I'm very anxious in the daytime or especially if I wake up from a nightmare, I rush into the corridor and call, "Mommy, Mommy, please come!" Yet I know perfectly well she's a thousand miles away. (She adds that her mother lives in the south of France where Georgette grew up and where her father died some 12 years ago.)
G At those times I'm convinced she's going to come to me. But what's even crazier, when she does come to stay with us I can't stand it. I'm in a state of constant tension. She has a way of looking at me as though I don't exist. She just wipes me out. Not long ago I plucked up the courage to tell her I felt she didn't love me or care about me and she replied, "Of course I do — why, I tell everyone what a clever man your husband is." When she does notice me, it's in a way that's sort of aggressive and erotic at the same time. She's always criticizing my appearance, telling me to rearrange my hair, not to wear bright clothing because I don't have the coloring for it . . . and so on. I just can't breathe when she's around. It's as though my whole

constant thoughts y mother, yet can't stand it when she come to me body might explode. Yet when she's not there I begin longing for her again. Do you think I'm crazy?

She appeared so distraught that I risked a small intervention.

JM You seem to be describing two different mothers that you carry around in your mind. There's the one you call on for comfort and reassurance and then there's this other one who wipes you out and won't let you breathe. Maybe these contradictory pictures of your mother seem crazy to you?

G Yes, isn't that odd. Even when I was little I clung to her all the time — not physically you understand. She didn't like to be touched, but I needed to know she was nearby — otherwise I felt I became transparent, just like when she comes to stay. I did everything I could to please her. I loved her so much. And I never cried in front of her because she couldn't stand it. I never ever let her know how afraid I was of falling to pieces. I had to stay alive, keep myself together by my own efforts.

In painting this rather striking portrait of her relationship with her mother, and how much she did out of love for her mother, Georgette seemed totally unaware of the hatred and despair that seeped through the words and metaphors she was using. In a slightly desperate tone of voice she asked me if I could find a place for her fairly soon. I reiterated what I had already told her on the phone, that I had no place for another year but that I would help her find an analyst once I knew a little more about her analytic project. At these words Georgette's face flushed deep scarlet; she began to tremble and appeared to have difficulty in breathing.

G I feel strange . . . my body is swelling up . . . please forgive me.

Touched by this mute somatic communication, I had a brief image of myself taking my patient, now a tiny child, into my arms and rocking her as though to reassure her that I would not "wipe her

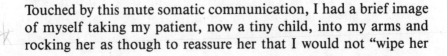

out," that her body would not explode. No doubt her desperate appeal for help and the black picture she had painted of her mother were unconsciously calculated to awaken just such countertransference reactions!

G Please don't cast me out. I'll wait as long as necessary.

I told her that we would need a second interview since many things were not clear to me and that we would decide at our next meeting whether or not it seemed advisable for her to wait another year.

At our next meeting Georgette brought two dreams in which I figured. In the first I was hugely pregnant and holding another child on my lap. She awoke from this dream in a state of acute anxiety. In the second I was playing with a little girl of about two years old, but this time she felt happy and peaceful. I learned during this consultation that Georgette was 15 months old when her first little sister was born; then, when she was nearly three, a second sister arrived. There were no other children.

The manifest content of the first dream already suggested a graphic representation of 15-month-old Georgette's memory, just before the birth of her sister, in which she feared that there was no longer any place for her. Did she feel "wiped out" by her mother after this birth, I wondered. In the second dream it might be supposed that Georgette was the two year-old girl, all alone at last, with the analyst-mother. I invited Georgette to tell me a little more about her early childhood.

G Well, I was always ill. (long pause) But that's not important. (silence)
JM Can you tell me something about the illness?
G I was seriously anorexic throughout my childhood and adolescence. Always being taken to doctors. Then I had bronchial asthma from the time I was very young. It stopped when I got married but it came back again after my little girl was born. Then I always had colds and sore throats. I still do . . . as well as asthma. But these things don't worry me.

With difficulty I got Georgette to tell me more about her somatic dysfunctioning. She "admitted" that she suffered from gastric ulcers and at other times from crippling rheumatic pain. But there was nothing to be alarmed over—she knew what she had to do when she was ill in these ways.

JM You seem to want to make light of these physical problems.
G I don't like talking about them. I always keep them hidden and never consult unless I really have to. In fact, I have a real phobia toward all medication—as though it will do me harm. I never take what is prescribed, so why consult?

Faced with my silence, which no doubt echoed a question, Georgette reluctantly described frightening tachycardia, adding that this was probably an hysterical manifestation since her father had died of a heart attack. There were also gynecological problems, but as with the cardiopathology, she was embarrassed to talk about these.

Although somewhat overwhelmed by Georgette's "organ recital," I noted that during this time she was able to look me straight in the eyes, almost defiantly, as though her string of illnesses were in some mysterious way reassuring to her. Did they form a protective shield that she did not wish to lose, that made her feel alive, as though her body and its functions truly belonged to her in illness? I was destined to wait many years before finding adequate replies to these and other queries. It already seemed clear to me that Georgette experienced herself as part of her mother's property. Perhaps only her body belonged to her, for I had the fleeting impression, at a certain moment, that she treated her physical ills as an erotic secret. A warning bell told me not to touch the vast psychosomatic dimension to Georgette's feeling of individual identity, so I made some meaningless remark to the effect that being ill could allow one to mother oneself, and perhaps being sick could even help one to feel "at home in one's skin." (The French expression, "être bien dans sa peau," means to feel both physically and mentally at ease.) This reference to her skin led Georgette to add a final touch to the multicolored psychosomatic portrait she had sketched for me.

G I have a number of skin allergies. Cat fur makes me itch all over, and some foods, especially fish and shellfish, make me swell up. Urticaria and more serious reactions. (She went on to describe symptoms resembling Quincke's edema and added that when this was localized in her throat it was frightening.) But this is inevitable. I inherited these allergies from my mother. She sometimes had to be hospitalized because of the violence of her reactions. Whenever my skin itched or swelled up she would say, "You're just like me."

I was to learn later that for Georgette this meant,"You *are* me — you don't exist." Perhaps this was one of the reasons that my patient's allergic propensities were the last to disappear from her body's variety theater in the course of this long analysis. They were a way of remaining erotically tied to her mother's body and mind and, as we shall learn later, the symbolic equivalent of combatting an unsuspected sexual tie to her father.

Perhaps at this point I was beginning to feel invaded, physically and mentally, by this final representation of Georgette's mother — or rather, by the profusion of mothers that seemed to inhabit her inner world. In any case, I pointed out that she had made little reference to her father, which is not something I would ordinarily do in first interviews; I usually tacitly agree to leave out of the picture that which the patient has, consciously or unconsciously, hidden from my view.

G Well, he was away a lot and my mother said such hideous things about him that it seemed impossible to love him. She always told me I disliked him and would never let him touch me or kiss me, even when I was very little. I do remember being terrified of him. Yet when he died I felt very shocked and hurt, especially as mother refused to let us talk about him or even look at the family photos after his death.

JM You did not think of them as a united couple?

G Oh no! My parents never shared the same bedroom. He lived in
   the far end of the house.

JM And you lived in the near end?

G Yes, with my mother and my sisters. And my grandmother too. I
   slept with her. I loved her very much. Always there, sitting in
   her wheelchair, for me to turn to. She watched over my Catholic upbringing. There were pictures of saints all over her bedroom wall and she would tell me their stories. She was an angel.

There is a saying in French to the effect that "angels have no sex."

JM An angel?

G Yes, I know. (Georgette gazed at the ground and spoke halt-
   ingly.) I cannot imagine that she ever had any sex life, ever. Her
   husband died shortly after their marriage and she never looked
   at another man.

   At this point I would like to add a relevant detail that I did not
learn until some three years later. I had presumed that the saintly
grandmother belonged to the maternal branch of the family, only
to learn with great surprise that she was the mother of Georgette's
father. There was an air of mystery about the mother-son relationship; as Georgette allowed herself to become aware of this she
became determined to discover more about her father's history.
She learned (what she had always known intuitively) that her father was the illegitimate child of a woman reputed to have been of
easy virtue and was subsequently adopted by the angel grandmother when he was still a baby. This may throw some light on what
Georgette next recounted concerning her father.

G I admired my father because he was so cultivated and encouraged us intellectually. But something terrible happened
   when I was 17. He read my secret diary and learned that I had
   had a very erotic flirtation with a boy. He thrashed me savagely
   for three days running. Beside himself, like a madman. I
   thought he was going to kill me. He kept screaming, "You're
   nothing but a whore! Just like your mother!"

While recounting this incident Georgette dropped her eyes to the ground, as though she too accused herself of being a whore. Her thoughts turned back to the angel grandmother.

G She never got angry with anyone. And I can't either.

It seemed already evident that Georgette had introjected not only the image of the saintly, sexless grandmother but also that of the whore-mother who had abandoned her father as a baby and whom she might come to represent in his eyes. Indeed she behaved like her violent and angry father to her own feminine self. In the same vein of condemnation of feminine desires, she went on to talk about her mother's attitude toward her.

G She wouldn't let me wear bright colors, said it made me look like a gypsy. I was the "dark one" of the family . . . like my father. I couldn't wear anything soft or lacy. No pink. She would mock me for my "little girl tastes." *She* could be seductive but it was dangerous for me. I don't know what my mother really wanted for me . . . I feel confused. In a way I didn't really exist except when she needed me to do so.

When I announced the end of the hour Georgette again became red, swollen and breathless. I believed that I was witnessing the prodromal signs of Quincke's edema, but today I would add that these were also undoubtedly physiological equivalents of affects of rage and terror. Georgette had not the slightest awareness of these emotions nor any mental representation to which they could be attached. Her psyche, while it had obviously sent out signals, was otherwise dormant at these times; only the physiological roots of these emotions remained visible.

I shall now give a few salient features of our first five years of work together. For two years Georgette cried ceaselessly throughout every one of her four-times-weekly sessions. She experienced her body as monstrous and uncontrollable, often falling, cutting or bruising herself, especially at the time of her periods or whenever any ideas concerning erotic feelings or feminine wishes would arise. In the sessions these were simply cast aside or mentioned in floods of tears with no further associations.

On the physical side Georgette was constantly besieged with septic sore throats, influenza, colds, gastric and cardiac dysfunctions, severe asthma, numerous anomalies in the functioning of her body fluids, and dermatological reactions of an allergic kind. Yet, no matter what pain or fever beset her, she never once missed a session, nor did she ever lament this continual state of ill-health. On the other hand, she complained bitterly of her *psychological* suffering in the analytic relationship. She dreaded the approach of every weekend. Each vacation break was heralded by anxiety dreams in which she was clinging to window ledges, suspended over a void, striving to maintain a grasp on crumbling cliffs, or struggling in tumultuous seas. At such times she clung even more avidly to the analysis, also clinging physically to the couch, burrowing into the cushions like a small animal suffering from the cold.

I shall leave aside the abundant material concerning Georgette's sexual and narcissistic fears in their more classical aspects, and concentrate instead on her specific way of experiencing her body and her relationship with me. She developed what might be termed a passionate maternal transference, which brought painfully to light profound homosexual longings and concomitant fears. But above and beyond these conflictual homosexual elements, there was a more primitive transference relationship that I came to call a transference *osmosis*. This included all that is described by Kohut (1971, 1977) as mirror transference and by Kernberg (1975, 1976, 1984) as pertaining to primitive emotional states. It reached a point where Georgette at times did not truly distinguish between my body and hers, nor between our personal identities. Of the many possible examples I could give, two will suffice.

Once when I returned from vacation, visibly sunburned, Georgette had a catastrophic reaction. "What have you done to my face?" she whimpered. She lost control of her movements and was too choked with emotion to speak for some five minutes. She finally whispered, "My face is hurting so badly." We were able to understand that, apart from the conviction that my face belonged to *her*, she also felt guilty beyond words, because in some way my burnt visage was her fault. As the session continued we were led to the conclusion that in fantasy Georgette believed she had attacked and devoured me with her infantile demandingness. In reply to my question, echoing her own, "What have you done to my face?" she told me that she was frequently terrified by the thought that her extreme dependence and demands upon me might cause me to fall ill. In all her dreams and fantasies around this time it became manifest that not only did we share the same face but there also was only *one body for the two of us*.

Small wonder that each impending vacation break caused Georgette's skin to erupt furiously in eczema-like manifestations accompanied by swellings, as well as burning or itching sensations which caused her considerable irritation and pain, as though with each separation her epidermis were torn away from mine. Yet at the same time these painful skin sensations were invested positively. In unconscious fantasy, whenever her own body was under attack mine too was attacked, which was my punishment for having abandoned her, a triumph, therefore, over the totally omnipotent mother who was felt to grant her no individual rights, either somatically or psychically. It now became evident that Georgette denied me my right to an individual body and a personal identity and life of my own.

This brings me to the second illustration of the osmotic transference and our indissoluble oneness. Georgette had occasionally met my husband coming into or leaving the building. One day she heard herself say, to her embarrassment, "A nice surprise. I just met our husband in the street." (It might be added that some years later she was torn apart with oedipal jealousies, but much analytic ground remained to be covered before that junction was reached.)

From here I shall concentrate mainly on Georgette's somatic "communications" and their slowly constructed unconscious significance. As her primitive fusional wishes and fears became more evident and able to be verbalized, in both their loving and their hating aspects, Georgette came into fuller possession of her feelings, particularly her growing awareness of violent negative affects towards her mother, her sisters, and — with much difficulty and fear — me.

Two years after the beginning of our work together Georgette appeared to be free at last of her ulcer pathology. There was no recurrence of it for the remaining seven years of her analysis. By the end of our third year she no longer suffered from asthma and her other respiratory disorders were remarkably less frequent. Although happy to feel well Georgette was also alarmed. "These changes worry me. If I no longer get asthma or catch colds or continue to create ulcers, it's as though I no longer exist." At the first level of interpretation I was able to put this into words for her: "If I no longer suffer physically, my mother will forget that I exist and you, the analyst-mother, will push me out of analysis."

A BODY THAT SUFFERS IS ALIVE

Much later a more profound significance, unconsciously attached to illness, revealed itself in a variety of ways. On one occasion Georgette remarked, "If my skin no longer swells and itches when I am about to separate from you, it's as though I would be without a skin and I'd fall to pieces. At least when I'm away from you I still know I have my skin. It speaks to me and reassures me that I live inside it." In other words, Georgette was reassured of her bodily integrity as well as her personal identity with each outbreak of neurodermatitis. The painful skin sensations also carried a further reassuring fantasy—that of taking something of my skin and presence with her. This was as surprising a discovery to me as to Georgette. In other words her suffering body performed the function of a *transitional object* (Winnicott, 1951) of a strange kind. Her burning skin gave her a feeling of being alive, of being held together, while at the same time recalling the memory of an outer object (the analyst and their "shared skin") that was reassuring to her. In my notes around this period I wrote, "A body that suffers is also a body that is alive."

But why did Georgette's body, her skin, and her somatic functioning have to do duty for a true transitional object? There was clearly a breakdown, as with many polysomatizing patients, in the early introjection of a soothing and caretaking mother image (Krystal, 1977, 1978a, 1978b) with which to identify. The positive investment in bodily suffering is reminiscent of those babies with incoherent mothering who bang their heads relentlessly on the sides of their cribs, as though to find confirmation of their body limits while distracting themselves from painful emotional states. What should have been supplied from internal sources (that is, some introjected image of the maternal environment that would restore to the infant a feeling of corporeal limits and of the capacity to contain painful emotional states) has to be sought *in the suffering body itself*.

On another occasion Georgette added a further dimension to the reassuring significance of physical suffering when she exclaimed, "I feel overwhelmed by this rage and hatred I feel toward my mother and my sisters. How did I not recognize it all these years? I'm afraid of this violence . . . that reminds me that the loss of most of my illnesses also frightens me. As long as my skin screamed and my stomach and bronchial tubes shouted, I knew I was alive. And so were the others! I hadn't killed anyone. My rage only hurt me."

We talked of her omnipotent fantasies and of what she imagined would happen if she allowed herself to become filled with feelings of rage and hatred. "I'm afraid it'll be like in childhood — that I'll go crazy and see signs of death everywhere, once again."

I began to suspect that genuinely psychotic symptoms may have alternated with psychosomatic ones during Georgette's childhood. However, she now became less afraid that the psychotic anxieties of her childhood years would reappear, and indeed came to see that for many years she had acted in accordance with such fears, which, once repressed, had given rise to many complicated character problems as well as a multitude of phobias. Prominent among the latter were fears of water, of flying, of enclosed spaces such as planes and elevators, of storms and thunder, as well as of many sights, sounds and odors that produced a catastrophic and disabling form of panic. (This list of psychological ills could be extended, and in fact, with the exception of certain comforting feelings connected with her physical suffering, Georgette was rarely free of mental suffering of one kind or another. This was, of course, part of her motivation for returning to analysis.)

As this material became interpretable and, therefore, could be worked over many times both in the transference and in childhood recollections, Georgette began to piece together more of her childhood somatic (and later sexual) theories. "My asthma stopped me from going mad. I remember creeping away with the feeling that I was facing death but that I would only be safe if I looked after myself. My mother penetrated me through every pore of my body! Her stare, her voice, her words, paralyzed me. And spelt death. Yet I had to cling to her, for somehow she represented life too."

The recognition that most of her phobic symptoms were secret scenarios intended to protect her from an "environmental" mother image with thundering, explosive and penetrating qualities led to the gradual disappearance of most of Georgette's phobias. As she was able to create within herself an image of a caretaking mother with soothing qualities, and thus become a better mother to the desperately frightened child within herself, her soma also abated its thundering and exploding. As may well be imagined, there was a wealth of anal-erotic and anal-sadistic fantasy behind these pregenital phobias, with their allied form of archaic sexual anxiety.

In spite of her fear of profound changes in her somatic self, Georgette's crippling rheumatic pain now recurred only at times of stress. The attacks of tachycardia, as well as her gynecological disturbances, would also reappear from time to time, but after interpretations of her lack of maternal care toward her own physical self and the slowly uncovered fantasy that these maladies were also a way of attacking my (her mother's) body at the same time, she agreed to consult a cardiologist and a gynecologist.

G I feel cold since most of my previous illnesses have gone. And I'm frightened of letting you see that they're disappearing.

JM As though, without your illnesses, you would no longer exist for me?

G It's true. I'm afraid of losing this identity of mine . . . in a way it's as though I always felt I existed because of my suffering body. It protected me against my mother's explosions and also against that other mother who wiped me out when I was no longer useful to her. And yet for some time now I feel I have the

courage to live in my own body, separated from you, and to let
you live in yours. Oh, my hands have become completely fro-
zen in telling you that!

JM In other words I will now abandon you, since I am only interested in you if you remain a part of myself?

G Yes! It's through my body's suffering that I keep this deep link
with you. What a strange idea!

A dream around this period (somewhere in the fifth year of
analysis) may serve to illustrate some of the above ideas.

G I dreamed that another woman and myself were together in an
elevator and we were both terrified of being trapped in it. Then
suddenly we were together in the bathroom. She had already
taken her bath and I had to bathe after her in the same water.
The water was covered with a most disgusting foam. I got in
but this foamy stuff stuck to my skin. I tried desperately to tear
it off and this woke me up.

Georgette began associating to the dream by remarking that
since waking she had gone back to a number of her old obsessional
rituals. To begin with, she had washed her hands all morning as
though they were dirty. She then detailed many other cleaning
rituals in which she frequently indulged but which she did not
regard as symptomatic. In fact, it seemed she wanted to show me
what a "nice clean girl" she was. (Later, masturbation guilt, as well
as sensuous associations to her mother's body, made this deeper
layer to the dream available for analysis.) She then remarked that
she had spent most of the afternoon trying to find a blouse in a
particular kind of material and was irritated by the fact that she
could neither remember the name of the material nor find the
blouse which would have "made her feel calm and comforted once
again."

Since Georgette seemed unconcerned by the earlier part of the
dream I began to gather my own associations, thinking that the
two women closed in the elevator might well represent Georgette
and myself locked together in our psychoanalytic relationship.

Only the day before she had reaffirmed that she would never want
to leave analysis and had had a reaction of panic when I tried to
interpret this babylike wish. When I reminded her of this she
agreed that she too had thought the two women in the elevator
might represent us — and concluded that the dream wish was that I
might share her phobia of being enclosed in elevators. This was no
doubt a genuine wish that we should be as one, with the same
thoughts and feelings. However, it seemed to me that the dream
was also putting on stage the *frightening* part of the desire to cling
to me forever, that is, frightening to the extent that I represented a
death-dealing internal mother from whom she longed to escape.
Although Georgette now recognized a constant feeling of rage
against her mother for having "made her a prisoner to her personal
needs," she was unable to attach these feelings to me in the
transference.

The bath foam which "stuck to her skin in a disgusting manner"
was reminiscent of the metaphors she used when expressing her
hatred of her mother's way of looking at her or rearranging her
hair and her clothing. I also wondered whether the feelings expressed in the dream and the subsequent hand-washing might provide a clue to possible archaic bodily fears underlying her numerous skin allergies, perhaps a glimpse into some mental recall of
primitive and as yet inexpressible fantasies. Since Georgette acknowledged the split images of the mother — the mother from
whom she longed to break away because she "spelt death" and the
mother to whom she wished to cling forever as the source of life
(now projected onto the analyst) — I tried to interest her in the
second part of the dream, which dealt with that highly invested
part-object, her skin.

JM And what about this sticky foam in our analytic bath?
G But coming here is like a breath of fresh air. I always go away
   feeling lighter and ready to live. Maybe it has to do with my
   mother . . . that way she had of looking at me, almost sexual,
   which made me feel as though she were attacking my body.
JM Perhaps we might learn more about those feelings here . . .
   you remember how often you felt uncomfortable lying on the

couch and you often wanted to cover up your body, as though I
too might look at you in that way?

G Yes. I know I'm still afraid to talk of sexual thoughts here, but
there's something worse. It's as though my body looks dirty
and deformed and I have to hide this from you.

Although these transference associations were too disturbing to
Georgette for her to continue with them, she did begin at this time
to allow a slightly different image of her mother to emerge.

G My mother is not a happy woman. In a way she's as stuck, as
locked into her relationship with me, as I am with her. Why do
I still suffer so badly from claustrophobia?

JM Well, you made this dream. Perhaps this babylike part of you
still wants to be locked in with her and to cling to her, like the
feelings you have here? Maybe it's easier to say this is her wish
rather than yours? Perhaps even the disgusting foam hides a
wish for her body and skin?

THE PARADOXICAL TRANSITIONAL OBJECT

The following day Georgette brought a confirmation of this last
interpretation, as well as an important forgotten memory.

G After the session I was thinking about the blouse that I couldn't
find in any of my favorite stores, and then I remembered a
beautiful nightgown of my mother's which was made of the
same material. The nightgown was very seductive and she kept
it in a locked drawer. It was made of that same soft foamy stuff
who's name I cannot remember. (I already guessed that it was
"crêpe georgette!") I wasn't allowed to touch it but she had a
handkerchief of the same material and she gave it to me. For a
long time I slept with it every night.

Apart from the fact that this memory added meaning to
Georgette's earlier choice of her pseudonym (since I had asked her
permission to quote parts of her analysis several months before the

session just recounted), it also put on the analytic stage her childhood attempts at creating a transitional object — the "foamy" crêpe
georgette handkerchief that represented (as do all pretransitional
objects) her mother's body, smell, and skin surface. But the striking piece of information supplied by the dream is that this same
foamy material was also *an object of horror*. In this way we may
suspect that the life-giving and death-dealing images of the mother
had never been truly separated into a desired and a feared object.
Instead they were coalesced, bearing witness to a breakdown in the
normal splitting processes of infancy. Nor had her transitional
object been able to fulfill its true function, namely, to liberate her
from her overdependence on her mother. Instead, to a certain
extent, her skin and bodily functions had to do duty for a genuine
transitional object. (I have frequently discovered this same disturbance in the formation of transitional phenomena in childhood
during the analysis of severely somatizing patients.) Georgette's
associations also threw light on the double reaction following her
dream: On the one hand she had been compelled to wash her
hands all morning as though to ward off unconscious fears of both
erotic and aggressive contact with her mother's body; on the other,
she had spent the afternoon looking for a metaphoric equivalent
of the good aspects of the mother's body, skin, and maternal
presence.

Perhaps this was one of the reasons for Georgette's somatic
reactions to certain situations that were both longed for and feared
at the same time. Her dermatological outbreaks were associated
with separation experiences, which meant life because they were
the proof of her independent existence, but also death because she
felt bereft and abandoned. Her edemic reactions to eating seafood,
which she longed for because "it looked and smelled so good" but
which made her gravely ill whenever she tried it, seemed to embody
the same paradoxical reaction. Although we had to wait for another year before the neurodermatitis and the edema yielded their
secrets, Georgette's airplane and elevator phobias finally disappeared around this time.

There were also many other changes. Georgette began to dress
in more colorful and feminine attire, she claimed to be more at

ease with her friends, and she made important progress in her professional work. In addition, her sex life became considerably more pleasurable and more important to her, although she still felt anxious about expressing such thoughts.

If I were to attempt to summarize the dynamic changes in the analytic relationship over these six years, I would say that the osmotic transference slowly became an anaclitic one, then a homosexual one, before becoming a truly oedipal one. Analysis of the homosexual transference led to Georgette's being able to envisage our being separated without danger to either of us. We were (almost) two individuals with individual bodies and identities. And her mother too began to aquire a different identity.

THE CHANGING MATERNAL IMAGO

A dream that occurred just before a vacation summed up, in a sense, the integration of Georgette's homosexual tie to her mother.

G I had one of those nightmares . . . just like in the old days when I still suffered from asthma. I was in a frail little boat and the sea grew angrier and angrier and I was going to be engulfed. But I found a small cabin to hide in. The sea kept climbing up the windows and thundering against them. Then suddenly I found there was a woman in my little house. She pointed to two pretty round-shaped pots that apparently were mine and said, "I want you to give me these." I didn't hesitate a second. I said, "Take them, they're yours!"

In recounting this part of the dream Georgette cupped her hands over her breasts and then stretched out her arms in a gesture that was evocative of her giving the "pots" to the woman. The thundering and threatening sea led her to think of her mother (in French, the identical sound of "mer" and "mère" lent weight to these equivalents) and to say that she felt she had rendered up all that was specifically hers — her femininity, her sexuality, her maternity — to her mother. I agreed with her proposed interpretation but added that in the dream theme she also "gave the breast" to her mother. (In French "donner le sein" is the common expression for breast-feeding.)

G But it's true! I used to "feed" her constantly — with little gifts and attentions. She needed attention the whole time to keep her together. I always felt guilty whenever she was sick or unhappy, as though it were my fault. I was her eternally devoted servant. She was my reason to exist. *She* was the lost child, not me!

Thus began the slow construction of a quite different maternal portrait — that of a narcissistically fragile woman, suffering from the same fear as Georgette herself, the fear that she could not exist as a separate individual. Indeed, it is possible that her mother's fragility was such that she used her children narcissistically to maintain an integrated image of herself, and that when they no longer fulfilled this function their needs and wishes ceased to exist in her eyes.

However this may be, the danger attached to Georgette's mental representation of her mother began to alter in character. Instead of feeling like "mother's little page-boy," as she once put it, she now sought to discover why she was in complicity with this role and had been able to protect herself from its dangers only through somatization.

G You once said I became grownup at 15 months. Did I tell you that I learned to walk when I was nine months old? Even then I was trying to get away, trying to manage on my own.

(We see here the tragedy of the precociously autonomous infant — a grownup shell that hides a small, symbiosis-seeking baby. Such children frequently fear success as adults, for this implies abandonment. We had often discussed Georgette's fear of achievement as well as of progress in the analysis — for this always meant that if she got better I would throw her out to die.)

G Always so independent, and yet I never realized that I lived my
   whole life in total submission to my mother. It was impossible
   to want anything she didn't want. But I am still astounded by
   the terrible hatred I have discovered for her . . . though it
   frightens me less than before. I feel now that my love feelings
   won't get destroyed by my rage.

Shortly after the appearance of these new themes Georgette
made a dream that heralded an important psychic change in her
internal universe. In dangerous cirumstances, she called out in her
dream "*Papa*, please come!" On awakening she felt strange, went
to look at herself in the mirror and, for the first time, discovered a
striking resemblance to her father!

Since my previous attempts to highlight the missing father in
Georgette's psychic world were rejected or immediately forgotten
by her, the introduction of her father as a highly invested object
was a significant psychic change and allowed for the first time a
glimpse into Georgette's oedipal organization as well as into the
early oedipal inhibitions which had, until now, bypassed the paths
of language. Thus, unacknowledged oedipal distress, although
registered by the psyche, could only be expressed in primitive,
somatopsychic ways. The following chapter will illustrate this important movement.

CHAPTER 11

Les Fruits de la Mère

NOW IN THE SEVENTH YEAR of analysis, Georgette began to look forward to vacation breaks, a feeling she had never experienced before. I should mention that, at this point in her analytic voyage, in spite of the disappearance of almost all her psychosomatic manifestations, she still suffered from severe allergic reactions whenever she ate certain fruits as well as fish and shellfish (known in French as "les fruits de mer" — allowing a play on words "the fruit of the mother"). I had come to call all these foods "the forbidden fruits."

G For the first time on vacation I felt happy with my body and at home in my skin ("bien dans ma peau"). No depression and no anxiety. And I'm not even afraid to tell you so! I only now realize fully what you have helped me to discover for so long — that my body belongs to nobody but me and that I need never again be afraid of its falling apart.

Before giving the rest of the session I should mention one other sign of the primitive "environmental" mother of infancy in Georgette's psychic structure: her acute awareness of odors (many of which originally appeared to cause allergic reactions). In the first years of analysis she constantly doused herself with perfume, partly to "stake out her territory" as I put it, because she always hoped that other patients would notice it (which indeed they did, often complaining that the odor clung even to the entrance of the building). There were also many anal-erotic and anal-sadistic fantasies attached to Georgette's need to be certain that no natural body odors were perceptible. Then, through dreams and associations, we came to discover that smell was closely linked also with sexual odors and a fear that the female sex had a disagreeable odor. On one occasion after tasting an oyster and consequently having a violent edemic reaction, Georgette dreamed about a woman's body in the form of a clam shell. In her associations she remembered that when she was a school child the slang word used by the village boys to refer to the girl's sex organ was "clam." Analysis of these important signifiers, while bringing significant changes in Georgette's enjoyment of her sexual relationship with her husband, had not effected any change in her violent allergic reactions. The latter, as we were to discover, were related to more archaic libidinal fantasies whose meaning had been foreclosed from consciousness.

In reflecting on the material, I thought to myself that tiny infants always seek the breast through their sense of smell, and that every baby surely knows the smell of its mother's sex, no doubt distinguishing the parents, among other signs, by their different *odors*. In thinking back over the analyses and childhood experiences of my "allergic" patients, I thought it probable that, even at this early stage of life, a propensity to allergic reactions might begin to be organized in the context of a disturbed mother-infant relationship. It also occurred to me that in many cases the toxic allergens had in infancy been smells, tastes or tactile experiences that were eagerly sought and invested *positively* by the infant.

In view of Georgette's extreme anxiety over the clam dream and its associations, as well as the approaching vacation, I attempted to interpret this material by saying that it seemed as though the little girl in her wanted to smell, to touch, to taste, and indeed to eat her mother's sex — as a primitive means of becoming her mother and possessing her sexual organ as well as her sexual privileges and imagined body contents.

There is little doubt in my mind that such incorporative fantasies, in which one becomes the other by eating either the person or the part that is desired, represent archaic libidinal longings of a universal kind. The persistence of these primitive erotic longings into adult life, in the form of psychosomatic manifestations, would indicate, once again, some early breakdown in the processes of internalization. I shall now leave it to Georgette to recount the use her psyche made of these tentative interpretations.

Les Fruits de Mer

G I've something important to tell you — I no longer have any allergies! During the vacation I ate everything — everything that is in the sea (mer and mère) — fish, oysters, lobsters, clams, mussels. I couldn't get enough. What a feast, and not the slightest allergic outbreak! I even ate strawberries and raspberries — everything that has made me suffer for the past 40 years.

There was a long silence before Georgette continued her associations.

G I thought of what you sometimes said about the "forbidden fruits" . . . my mother's fruit, her breasts, her sex, her babies . . . that some little girl in me wanted to devour, so I could become a woman. It feels profoundly true and I don't know why the idea frightened to me for so many years. (another silence) One day I was talking enthusiastically to my husband about how much I now love the "fruits de mer" and instead I said, "How I love the fruits de père!"

This slip of the tongue attributes the forbidden fruit to the father as well as the mother — a most important and, in spite of our combined efforts, missing dimension in Georgette's psychic world. I asked Georgette to explore this interesting idea further, and she brought back a lost memory.

G How strange . . . how could I have forgotten? My father adored fish and shellfish. He swallowed them all with great gusto — mussels, shrimp, clams, oysters. Oh! I've remembered something else. I must have been about three. I was watching my father with great fascination, eating a clam or a mussel. And he offered me one. I can still see it. He separated the two little . . . er, the two little parts (I nearly said "the two little lips") . . . and he squeezed a drop of lemon-juice into it and gave it to me to eat. I swallowed it down and it was delicious! How come I didn't remember all these years that shellfish were my father's passion? Seafood was his special territory!

Struck by Georgette's use of evocative metaphors concerning her father's "passion" and "territorial rights," I decided to interpret the image of the primal scene which she had painted for me with the surrealistic vision of a child's eye: The father's opening the shellfish and depositing a drop of lemonjuice therein.

JM The little lips of the shellfish and the drop of lemon juice — could this be a childlike image of your two parents together?
G I feel confused . . . everything is getting mixed up in my mind . . .
JM Father and mother?
G Yes! And that special smell . . . my father had a smell that frightened me. *That's* why I wouldn't let him kiss me when I was a schoolchild! That's another thing I'd forgotten. Now I'm thinking of something that embarrasses me. . . . My father who ate shellfish all the time — is this crazy? — would have the smell of my mother's sex. . . . But there's another thought that's even harder to say. Well, here goes! I was telling my friend Eva yesterday about my great discovery of the female sex and the shellfish and she replied that sperm also smells of shrimp.

JM The "fruit of the sea." . . . where both sexes meet? Is that the thought that is difficult to say?

At this point I reminded Georgette how often she had talked of the persecuting quality of odors and said that it now seemed evident that she refused the sexual odors and especially their implication that her parents existed as a sexual couple. The rituals of closing her mouth, holding her breath, and so on, that she had practiced secretly throughout her childhood, were no doubt intended, as she always affirmed, to ward off death, but we might wonder whether they were not equally directed to denying the sexual relationship between her parents — which to the little Georgette of the past was no doubt experienced as a threat of death.

G Yes, I'm beginning to see this!
JM To look?
G Yes and to understand . . . the odor! It was the smell of their room that I had to avoid at all costs!

Thus for the first time in seven years Georgette was able to recognize that her parents slept together in the same bed, at least until she was three. At that moment she also recalled a dream she had made in the first week of her analysis with me. She was looking at a pair of earrings in crystal and was not able to put them on. Since this was one of her first dreams, I had picked up on "pair," "ears," "earrings," her "looking," being unable to "use" the earrings, etc., but no further associations came to her mind. Now she proclaimed with delight, "I know what those crystal drops were — the beads that decorated the lamps in their bedroom!"

Thus a new and vital link had now been forged in the chain of forgotten memories in Georgette's inner world. The oedipal dimension could finally be added to all that we had already been able to reconstruct of Georgette's passionate love-hate attachment to her mother's body and person. The narcissistic mortification and despair that the little Georgette had undoubtedly experienced at the birth of her sisters were now encapsulated in the forgotten memory — a screen memory, destined to be repressed — in which her father enjoys avidly (under the guise of the "fruits of the sea") the mother's sex, giving rise to their mutual fruit, the little sisters.

Faced with her own infantile wish to eat her mother (which for all children represents the first fantasy attempt to internalize and libidinally possess the mother universe), the amorous little cannibal could turn neither to mother nor to father for any confirmation that she too would be a woman one day and would have the right to sexual desires and sexual fulfillment. For many reasons — of which I have indicated a few — Georgette had "no place" to go. There was no model of a loving couple within which to discover her own future as a woman. In the first place, her need to introject her mother's image as a narcissistically reassuring representation of femininity had failed, later blocking the integration of normal homosexual wishes (since any attempt to draw close to her mother brought her into the field of her mother's narcissistic needs, where she could at any moment be disinvested or feel her own individual existence to be denied). In addition, she believed her mother had forbidden her to love her father; thus she was unable to turn to him, as most small children do, for help in disengaging herself from the primitive love-hate tie to her mother.

After the birth of her little sister, which almost certainly brought about a sudden disinvestment of Georgette in her mother's eyes, any attempt on the little girl's part to cling to her psychically absent mother would be experienced as doubly dangerous: On the one hand her demand for fusional oneness spelt psychic death; on the other she was terrified of her own destructive wishes, fearing that she might omnipotently destroy father, mother, and the little sisters — fruit of the mother's womb and the father's seed — and consequently lose her own right to live. These fantasies were now buried in the taste of raspberries and strawberries, and in the smell of shellfish and seafood (the parents' sexual odors and relationship), their taste and smell being impregnated with the body memories and archaic libidinal longings of an infant, and only secondarily acquiring verbal and oedipal significance. In other words these "forbidden foods" were *symbolic equivalents* (Segal, 1957) and not *signifiers* for the different aspects of the "breast mother" of early infancy.

Without the earlier substratum of psychological distress, *these same elements might have been used to create hysterical and not psychosomatic symptoms.* The forgotten memory of the father, with all it epitomized for the little girl of the primal scene and his phallic role in the parental couple, could scarcely of itself have produced the severe psychosomatic regression that had dogged Georgette's life, had the earlier relationship to the mother not been so perturbed. The preverbal signifiers of the early relationship, as yet incapable of verbal symbolization, had given rise to "symbolic equations" which Segal (1957) likened to a psychotic mechanism, or again could be said to possess merely the status of a "picto-gram" (Aulagnier, 1975) or, in Bion's terminology, of "beta ele-ments" (1963). The psyche, short-circuiting word-presentations through the regression to infantile ways of experiencing mental pain, was left with dynamic but destructive thing-presentations (Freud 1915a, 1915b, 1916–1917) with which to function and emit warning signals. Since they were not contained in words, such thing-presentations mobilized powerful and uncontrollable uncon-scious forces whenever the psyche detected a menacing situation (such as separation experiences or feelings of rage).

To these mute warnings were later added oedipal interdictions of both a homosexual and a heterosexual nature. The latter, having achieved verbal representations, were subsequently repressed, and thereafter were to provide a fund of elements to furnish later neu-rotic symptoms (such as Georgette's multiple phobias and obses-sive rituals). However, any transgression of Georgette's *archaic* incestuous longings, in the form of the wish to eat the "forbidden fruits," could rely on no defensive neurotic barriers of this kind and thus risked causing a somatic explosion as had occurred in her early infancy, when psychic distress could respond only to the mental representation of bodily sensations. These somatic ills were later invested with sadistic fantasies turned against her own body and self. The amorous and destructive infantile wishes that Georgette's analytic exploration had painfully brought to light were kept completely hidden from conscious and even precon-scious awareness. But, as Freud (1923) so aptly observed, *affects may readily bypass the preconscious layers of mental functioning.*

We can thus understand that in the face of disturbing affect Georgette's psyche could give only primitive somatopsychic signals.

On the other hand, the complex knot of anguish, marked by dangerous loving and hating impulses, as well as the usual oedipal interdictions, while these also remained out of reach of psychic representation and its subsequent elaboration, had undergone a different psychic development. Their profound repression gave rise instead to a series of hysterophobic and phobo-obsessional defenses; they formed part of the conscious suffering for which Georgette sought psychoanalytic help.

As for the psychosomatic component in Georgette's psychic structure, this psychic compromise illustrates well the notion of an archaic form of hysteria, in which the struggle is fundamentally directed, not to preserving one's genital sexuality (as in the classical concept of hysteric structure), but to protecting life itself as expressed through the early libidinization of the whole somatic self. These vital elements in Georgette's psychic structure were excluded from the symbolic chain of language and thus had to be painfully recreated through the analytic process.

Might we not suppose that, in the face of anguish and mentally irrepresentable despair, the massive but unelaborated messages that the psyche was able to send short-circuited the structures of language? Consequently, the psyche's messages were decoded as an injunction to the soma to throw its forces blindly into the struggle against psychic pain. Something similar happens in infancy when a nursling, through its cries, bodily gestures and somato-psychic reactions to stress, gives nonverbal communications that only a mother is able to interpret. She functions, in this respect, as her baby's thinking system, and finds an adequate response to her infant's distress. Due to some breakdown in the introjective processes of infancy, in which the baby slowly comes to create in its inner world a representation of this maternal function with which to identify, this fundamental psychic structure is faulty. Patients like Georgette have maintained the body-mind link, characteristic of babyhood, at this presymbolic level.

We might wonder why certain forms of somatic dysfunctiong

are chosen in preference to others. This question is too vast to be explored adequately here; nevertheless, we might single out the importance of chance encounters between body and mind at certain important moments during the early structuring of the psyche. When, for example, the mind is searching for some representation of a threatening situation in order to give out an appropriate signal of action to be taken, it may happen that the body, due either to illness or innate somatic vulnerabilites (such as the allergies from which Georgette's mother suffered), becomes mentally connected with the danger signal emitted by the psyche. It is evident that the body has a tenacious memory of its own.

When such a conjunction is established during the early structuring of the psyche such pathological psychosomatic links may last a lifetime, offering the individual no means, other than drastic somatization, of reacting to external and internal stress since these are excluded from more evolved forms of mental representation and affect-recognition. To take a simplified example, we might imagine that when an infant holds its breath at times of severe anxiety, this may constitute a future basis for the symptoms of bronchial asthma; the asthmatic reaction may then arise, in any situation that arouses anxiety, in place of a word-presentation linked to the anxious affect that would render the experience accessible to thought, thereby circumventing a direct somatic response to the psyche's warning message.

It follows from these hypotheses that psychosomatic maladies, even of a life-threatening nature, might, paradoxically, be used in the service of psychic survival.

In Georgette's case this survival technique required her to stifle all hostile thoughts, to whatever degree, aroused against her first love objects. In order to maintain disinvested and disembodied links with both parents, the distressed psyche appeared to have no means of expression other than sending primitive impulses of a "flight or fight" order which resulted in multiple forms of somatic dysfunctioning. In place of a *psychosexual* history, Georgette presented a *psychobiological* one; her unrecognized emotional conflicts were manifested first in the grave anorexia that lasted throughout her childhood and adolescence, then in the serious refusal to breathe expressed in her asthmatic attacks from baby-hood onward. To these were added the mute rebellion that resulted in heart pathology, gynecological disturbance, ulcers, edemic reactions and neurodermatitis. Georgette believed that the desired-and-feared fantasy that there was only one body for two was her mother's law. Any refusal to comply with this law would incur the loss of her mother's love and, therefore, psychic death. She proved able to reassure herself, through her body's suffering, that she need not be afraid of the destructive aspects of this wish, which threatened both her bodily integrity and her individual identity.

Might we not conclude that all Georgette's psychosomatic manifestations conveyed her profound determination to survive? Meanwhile, her constant somatic productions on the psychoanalytic stage obliged us to decode the soma's mute "communications" and to translate these primitive messages into verbalizable psychic representations. The "*bio*-logic" that ruled Georgette's body-mind functioning was slowly transformed into "*psycho*-logic," enabling her anarchic and ahistorical body, over the long years of analysis, at last to became a symbolic one, and her mind to be freed from its psychosomatic chains.

With the story of Georgette this book comes to a close. I have attempted to give my readers a glimpse into the way one psychoanalyst has learned to listen to the body's "language," a language that has many "dialects." As may be seen throughout this book, each patient, using the soma's complex translation of the psyche's messages, reveals a different drama. When its theme can be told, and shared, in the therapeutic situation—for the work of analysis is always a story recreated by two people—the mind is able to take over the task of modifying the drama. In so doing, the body becomes relieved of its repetitive attempts to find a solution to psychic pain.

Nevertheless, the factors that produce psychic change constantly elude us. This book gives rise to more questions than answers. It is my hope that my colleagues will share their insights with me, and that our efforts, combined with the findings from other disciplines concerned with the body-mind link and its mysteries, may fruitfully advance our knowlege of the psychosomatic self.

Bibliography

Alexander, F. 1950. *Psychosomatic medicine*. New York: Norton. Re-issued 1987.

Alexander, F., French T., and Pollock, G. (Eds.) 1968. *Psychosomatic specificity*. Chicago: University of Chicago Press.

American Heart Association, Heart Facts Reference Sheet, 1978.

Aulagnier, P. 1975. *La violence de l'interprétation*. Paris: Presses Universitaires de France.

Bion, W. 1959. Attacks on linking. In *Second thoughts*. London: Heinemann, 1967, pp. 93–109.

_____. 1962. *Elements of psychoanalysis*. London: Heinemann.

_____. 1963. *Learning from experience*. London: Heinemann.

Breuer, J. and Freud, S. 1893–95. *Studies on hysteria*. Standard Ed. 2: London: Hogarth Press, 1955.

Brazelton, T. 1982. Joint regulation of neonate-parent behavior. In *Social interchange in infancy*, ed. E. Tronick. Baltimore Md.: University Park Press.

Dunbar, F. 1943. *Psychosomatic diagnosis*. New York: Hoeber Press.

173

Engel, G. 1962. Anxiety and depression withdrawal: The primary affects of unpleasure. *International Journal of Psycho-analysis* 43: 89–97.

Fain, M. 1971. *Prélude à la vie fantasmatique*. Revue Française de Psychanalyse. 35: 291–364.

Fain, M., Kreisler L., and Soulé, M. Paris: 1974. *L'enfant et son corps*. Presses Universitaires de France.

Ferenczi, S. 1931. Child analysis in the analysis of adults. In *Final Contributions*. London: Hogarth Press, 1955.

Freud, S. 1898. Sexuality in the aetiology of the neuroses. Standard Ed. 3: 263–285. London: Hogarth Press, 1962.

_____. 1900. The interpretation of dreams. Standard Ed. 5: 509–622. London: Hogarth Press, 1953.

_____. 1911a. Psychoanalytic notes on an autobiographical account of paranoia. Standard Ed. 12: 9–79. London: Hogarth Press, 1957.

_____. 1911b. Formulations on the two principles of mental functioning. Standard Ed. 12: 219–220. London: Hogarth Press, 1957.

_____. 1914. On narcissism: An introduction. Standard Ed. 14: 67–102. London: Hogarth Press, 1957.

_____. 1915a. Repression. Standard Ed. 14: 146–158. London: Hogarth Press, 1957.

_____. 1915b. The unconscious. Standard Ed. 14: 159–216. London: Hogarth Press, 1957.

_____. 1916–17. The common neurotic state. Standard Ed. 16: 378–391. London: Hogarth Press, 1963.

_____. 1918. From the history of an infantile neurosis. Standard Ed. 17: 13–122. London: Hogarth Press, 1955.

_____. 1920. Beyond the pleasure principle. Standard Ed. 18: 7–61. London: Hogarth Press, 1955.

_____. 1923. The Ego and the Id. Standard Ed. 19: 3–59. London: Hogarth Press, 1962.

_____. 1924. The loss of reality in neurosis and psychosis. Standard Ed. 19: 183–190. London: Hogarth Press, 1961.

_____. 1937. Constructions in analysis. Standard Ed. 23: 255–270. London: Hogarth Press, 1964.

_____. 1938a. Splitting of the ego in the process of defense. Standard Ed. 23: 271–278. London: Hogarth Press, 1957.

_____. 1938b. An outline of psychoanalysis. Standard Ed. 23: 144–194. London: Hogarth Press, 1964.

Friedman, M. and Rosenman, R. 1959. Association of specific behavior pattern with blood and cardiovascular findings. *Journal of the American Medical Association.*

Gaddini, R. 1970. Transitional objects and the process of individuation: a study in three different social groups. *Journal of the American Academy of Child Psychiatry.* vol. 9: 2.

_____. 1975. The concept of transitional object. *Journal of the American Academy of Child Psychiatry.* vol. 14: 4.

Green, A. 1973. *Le Discours Vivant.* Paris: Presses Universitaires de France.

Kernberg, O. 1975. *Borderline conditions and pathological narcissism.* New York: Jason Aronson.

_____. 1976. *Object relations theory and clinical psychoanalysis.* New York: Jason Aronson.

_____. 1984. *Severe personality disorders.* New Haven: Yale University Press.

Klein, M. 1935. Contribution to the psychogenesis of manic-depressive states. *Contributions to Psychoanalysis* (1921–1945), pp. 382–410. London: Hogarth Press, 1950.

Kohut, H. 1971. *The Analysis of the Self.* New York: International Universities press.

_____. 1977. *The restoration of the self.* New York: International Universities Press.

Krystal, H. 1977. Aspects of affect theory. *Bulletin of the Menninger Clinic* 41: 1–26.

_____. 1978a. Trauma and affects. *Psychoanalytic Study of the Child* 36: 81–116.

_____. 1978b. Self-representation and the capacity for self-care. In *Annual of Psychoanalysis* 9: 93–113. New York: International Universities Press.

Lacan, J. 1966. *Ecrits.* Paris: Seuil

Lewin, B. 1946. Sleep, the mouth and the dream screen. In *The Yearbook of Psychoanalysis*, 3. New York: International Universities Press. 1947.

_____. 1948. Inferences from the dream screen. In *The Yearbook of Psychoanalysis*, 6. New York: International Universities Press. 1950.

Lichtenstein, H. 1961. *The dilemma of human identity.* New York: Jason Aronson. 1977.

McDougall, J. 1964. Homosexuality in women. In *Female sexuality*, ed. J. Chasseguet. Ann Arbor: University of Michigan Press, 1974.

_____. 1972. The anti-analysand in analysis. In *Ten Years of Psycho-analysis in France*. New York: International Universities Press, 1980.

_____. 1978. *Plea for a measure of abnormality*. New York: International Universities Press, 1980.

_____. 1982a. *Theaters of the mind: Illusion and truth on the psychoanalytic stage*. New York: Basic Books, 1985.

_____. 1982b. Alexithymia: a psychoanalytic viewpoint. *Psychotherapy and Psychosomatics*. 38: 81–90.

_____. 1982c. Alexithymia, psychosomatisis and psychosis. *International journal of psychoanalysis and psychotherapy*. 9: 379–388.

_____. 1986. Identifications, neoneeds and neosexualities. *International Journal of Psycho-analysis* 67, 19: 19–31.

McDougall, J. and Lebovici, S. 1960. *Dialogue with Sammy*. London: Hogarth Press. 1969.

Mahler, M., Bergman, A., and Pine, F. 1975. *The Psychological birth of the human infant*. New York: Basic Books.

Marty, P. de M'Uzan, M., and David, C. 1963. *L'investigation psychosomatique*. Paris: Presses Universitaires de France.

Marty, P. and de M'Uzan, M. 1963. La pensée opératoire. *Revue Française de Psychanalyse* 27: 1345–1356.

Montgrain, N. 1987. The words of madness. Paper presented at the 35th International Psychoanalytical Congress, Montreal, July 1987.

Nemiah, J. 1978. Alexithymia and psychosomatic illness. *Journal of Continuing Education in Psychiatry*, pp. 25–37.

Nemiah, J. and Sifneos, P. 1970. Affect and fantasy in patients with psychosomatic disorders. *Modern Trends in Psychosomatic Medicine*, vol. 2. London: Butterworth.

Ogden, T. 1980. The nature of schizophrenic conflict. In *Projective Identification and Psychotherapeutic Technique*, pp. 135–171. New York: Jason Aronson, 1982.

_____. 1986. *The matrix of the mind: Aspects of object relations theory*. New York: Jason Aronson.

_____. 1988. On the concept of an autistic-contiguous position. *International Journal of Psychoanalysis*. (in press).

Osler, W. 1910. Angina Pectoris, Lancet. 2: 839.

Pascal, B. 1670. Pensées, 4. Paris: Jean de Bonnot. 1950.

Rosenman R., Brand R., Jenkins C., Friedman T., Straus R., and Wurm M. 1975. *Coronary heart disease: Final follow-up experiment of eight and one-half years*. 233 p. 832.

Segal, H. 1957. Notes on symbol formation. *International Journal of Psychoanalysis* 38: 391–397.

Sifneos, P. 1975. Problems of psychotherapy in patients characteristics and physical disease. *Psychotherapy and Psychosomatics* 26: 65–70.

Stern, D. 1985. *The interpersonal world of the infant.* New York: Basic Books, 1958.

Winnicott, D. 1951. Transitional objects and transitional phenomena. In *Collected Papers*, pp. 229–42. New York: Basic Books.

_____. 1965. *The maturational process and the facilitating environment.* London: Hogarth Press.

_____. 1971. *Playing and reality.* New York: Basic Books.

Index

action, as defense, 94–95, 97
"acting out", 95
"activity addiction", 97
addictive behavior, 19, 27, 43, 90, 94–98,
    101, 124
  cigarette smoking as, 134–35
  sexuality as, 98–100
  as transitional object, 82–89
affect(s), 90–105, 107, 168
  dispersal of, 94–98
  lack of, 23, 91, 93–94, 101, 130–31
  metapsychology of, 44
  in psychosis, 114
  pulverized, 104
  stifled, 64–65
  see also disaffectation
"affect-equivalents", 104
affect pathology, 111
alcoholism, 83, 87
  as affect dispersal, 94–95
Alexander, F., 18
alexithymia, 24–25, 37, 93, 95, 103
allergies, 13–14, 84, 147, 158, 162, 163
angina pectoris, 14, 21
  see also cardiopathology
anorexia, childhood, 145, 170
"anti-analysands", 93
anxiety, 96
  archaic, 74
"archaic hysteria", 20, 54, 55
asthma, 23, 55, 83, 84, 145, 154, 170, 171
Aulagnier, P., 47, 168
autism, 43
autonomy, early, 26, 46, 160

babies, *see* infants
Bergman, A., 41

Bion, W., 39, 41, 114, 117, 168
body:
  disavowal of zones, functions, 47
  "language" of, 12, 171
  overfunctioning, 18
  as plaything of the mind, 19–20
body-mind relationship, 14, 28, 32–49, 64,
    101–2, 171
Brazelton, T., 26
breast-mother, 65, 96, 115, 167
"breast-universe", 33, 34
Breuer, J., 1, 16

cardiopathology, 21–22, 25–26, 126, 129,
    146
castration anxiety, 36–37
castration fantasies, 99–100
causality, 101
  precipitating vs. underlying, 19–20
change:
  fear of, 8, 92, 116, 131
  resistance to, 93
"Chicago seven" (bronchial asthma,
    gastric ulcer, essential hyper-
    tension, rheumatoid arthritis,
    ulcerative colitis, neuroder-
    matitis, thryotoxicosis), 18
communication, symbolic, 34–35
compensation, 52
"cork-child", and chasmic mother, 78
coronary heart disease, 21–22, 25–26
  see also cardiopathology
countertransference, 8, 10–11, 117, 145
  and disaffected patient, 90, 92, 100, 115,
    116, 126–27
  negative, 109
crying, 121, 123

179